1

D1644468

INTERNATIONAL ADOPTION

AUSTRALIA

The Law Book Company
Brisbane • Sydney • Melbourne • Perth

CANADA

Carswell
Ottawa • Toronto • Calgary • Montreal • Vancouver

Agents

Steimatzky's Agency Ltd, Tel Aviv;
N.M. Tripathi (Private) Ltd, Bombay;
Eastern Law House (Private) Ltd, Calcutta;
M.P.P. House, Bangalore;
Universal Book Traders, Delhi;
Aditya Books, Delhi;
MacMillan Shuppan KK, Tokyo;
Pakistan Law House, Karachi, Lahore

INTERNATIONAL ADOPTION

By

JEREMY ROSENBLATT
Barrister, Gray's Inn Chambers

LONDON
SWEET & MAXWELL
1995

347.4261 R

Published in 1995 by
Sweet & Maxwell Limited of
South Quay Plaza, 183 Marsh Wall,
London E14 9FT
Phototypeset by LBJ Enterprises of Aldermaston and Chilcompton.
Printed and bound in Great Britain by The Alden Press Ltd, Oxford.

No natural forests were destroyed to make this product.
Only farmed timber was used and replanted.

**A catalogue record for this book is
available from the British Library**

ISBN 0 421 52 770 6

All rights reserved. UK statutory material in this
publication is acknowledged as Crown copyright.
No part of this publication may be
reproduced or transmitted, in any form
or by any means, or stored in any retrieval
system of any nature, without prior written permission,
except for permitted fair dealing under the Copyright,
Designs and Patents Act 1988, or in accordance with
the terms of a licence issued by the Copyright
Licensing Agency in respect of photocopying and/or
reprographic reproduction. Application for permission
for other use of copyright material including
permission to reproduce extracts in other published
works shall be made to the publishers. Full acknowledgement
of author, publisher and source must be given.

The index was prepared by Jeanne Bradbury

17 JUL 1995

©
J. Rosenblatt
1995

For my sister, Tessa and her daughter, Lotte.

Acknowledgement

The Overseas Adoption Helpline and the British Association for Fostering and Adoption are thanked for their assistance.
Karen Davies of White & Sherwin, Solicitors, is thanked for kindly checking through the manuscript.

CONTENTS

Contents

INTRODUCTION

The importance of adoption is enshrined internationally in the United Nations Declaration of Human Rights, Art. 16, which concerns the right to found a family, even an international family, and in the United Nations Declaration on Social and Legal Principles Relating to the Welfare of Children, which confirms that the best interest of the child, particularly his or her need for affection and the security of continuing care should be the paramount consideration. These, and other international treaties and conventions relating to adoption, can be found in Appendix 1 to this work.

At present, the procedure for bringing a child into England and Wales from abroad, with the intention of adopting that child, brings together two areas of law, Family and Immigration. Until there is proper regulation by statute, these two areas can clash inexorably, leaving a child in an unwelcome state of limbo, between two countries.

More commonly known as inter-country adoptions, international adoptions are not always inter-country *per se*, in that they do not always involve the respective procedures of two separate countries, though that is the preferable method for such applications. A child's habitual residence of origin, will, needless to say, usually be a country other than England and Wales in such applications. However, adoptions of an international nature have not always come into being through inter-country recognised procedure, be it set down in statute form or not.

Some adoptions have occurred when "foreign" children have been abandoned in England and Wales; others when parents from abroad with only limited leave to remain in England and Wales, have given their "foreign" children, with the same indefinite immigration status as their own, voluntarily up for adoption in England and Wales. Whilst adherence to the adoptive legal requirements of the child's country of origin ought to have been made prior to a domestic adoption application, an adoption order of England and Wales can only come into being through the domestic process of its courts. These are just some reasons why this book is entitled International Adoption and not Inter-Country Adoption.

At present, whatever type of foreign adoption order has been obtained, be it from a designated country under the Adoption (Designation of Overseas Adoptions) Order 1973 or a Convention country (see Chap. 1, below, for definitions), an application may still have to be made to the court of England and Wales, depending upon the Home Secretary and the immigration status of the child. A declaration can be sought in accordance with the Adoption Act 1976, s.39, that the applicant child is already adopted by the applicants (see App. 3E) through a foreign court, but before the court of England and Wales will make such a declaration it is going to have to be satisfied, as with all other international adoptions, that requirements have been met under ordinary domestic law relating to adoption. There would appear to be no easy way round the law which at present demands recourse to the

1

domestic procedure even if there has already been conscientious consideration of the application by the foreign court.

All that will change as soon as the Hague Convention on Intercountry Adoption 1993 ("the 1993 Convention"; set out in App. 1C) becomes law, if and when a new Adoption Act comes into being. The proposed Adoption Act will incorporate the Hague Convention into domestic law just as the Child Abduction and Custody Act 1985 ratified the Hague Convention on the Civil Aspects of International Child Abduction 1984 ("the 1984 Convention").

The 1993 Convention will prevent the present duplication of proceedings in different countries. Signatories will have shown that their domestic procedure for dealing with adoptions of an international nature, with all the investigative requirements involved, is of a sufficiently high and acceptable standard to deem the duplication of the adoption application unnecessary.

The 1984 Convention deals with what to do after a particular event, namely the abduction of a child, whilst the 1993 Convention deals with matters leading up to an event, namely the adoption of a child into or from England and Wales. A central authority, under the probable auspices of the Department of Health, will deal with international adoption applications on an inter-country basis, just as the Official Solicitors' Department under the Lord Chancellor's Department deals with child abduction matters. The new central authority will co-ordinate applications in England and Wales with the sending country abroad, delegating to local authorities who will furnish their homestudy assessment report, before gaining entry clearance for any child through the immigration authorities at the Home Office. Such a central authority in its co-ordinating role will seek to ensure that applications are dealt with smoothly, ensuring most importantly that duplication of adoption proceedings need not take place.

Whilst not wishing to sound unnecessarily pessimistic regarding an international convention which has great merit, it could be some time before there is a new Adoption Act incorporating the 1993 Convention and, if incorporated, it might take even more time before its process does indeed run smoothly.

As an example, The Hague Convention on Jurisdiction, Applicable Law and Recognition of Decrees relating to Adoption 1965 (see App. 18), was ratified in England and Wales in 1978, but, extraordinarily, the only other signatories are Austria and Switzerland, despite the effluxion of time. So far as the 1993 Convention is concerned, countries may not get around to incorporating the new Convention into their domestic law, despite being a signatory. It is for this reason that the procedures laid down in this book, dealing with the presently required duplication of proceedings, will not become so readily redundant.

In addition, the procedures set out in this book will probably still be necessary for those adoptions of an international nature involving children who arrive in England and Wales without prior immigration clearance, or as stated, those children who are given up voluntarily or abandoned to local authorities by foreign parents.

As has been said, one of the problems of adoptions of an international nature is the conflict between family law and immigration law.

There have been situations where foreign courts have granted applicants the right to adopt a child, with leave to remove that child from the jurisdiction, only to discover that entry clearance into England and Wales has been refused. The new Convention will incorporate such immigration requirements into its workings: a child will not be able to be adopted for the purpose of removal abroad by the sending country, unless and until entry clearance has been granted into the receiving country.

The information contained in this book derives from statute in terms of domestic applications but relies upon Home Office guidelines, if not word-of-mouth, regarding international procedures for locating a child then seeking to bring him into England and Wales for the purpose of adoption: they do not necessarily have a statutory base because, at present, no statute exists as a guide. A special agreement does exist with Romania which came into force on May 5, 1992 (see App. 1H). It is suggested in this book that adoption applications of an international nature be set down in the High Court, but there is nothing to prevent them being set down in the County Court, and then transferred if they are legally grave or weighty in their content, in accordance with *Practice Direction (Adoption: Transfer of Proceedings)* [1994] 1 W.L.R. 13 (see App. 5); and see *Re N and L* [1987] 1 W.L.R. 829. For the sake of clarity, a child, is referred to in the masculine in the text and prospective adoptive applicant parents as "the applicants". Adoption agencies are stated as being local authorities alone, which is likely to be the case under the new convention although presently a voluntary adoption agency could prepare the homestudy assessment report.

Jeremy Rosenblatt
Gray's Inn Chambers

Chapter 1

THE TYPES OF INTERNATIONAL ADOPTION

There are a number of different types of adoption possessing an international element. Those most commonly encountered are inter-country and Convention adoptions. The difference between the types of adoption depends upon the legal recognition of their coming into being by the English court. Thus Convention adoptions are so-called because they are adoptions in countries whose systems are recognised in England by reason of an international convention, whilst an adoption in India, for example, will not have the same standing because India is not a signatory to such a treaty. It is the English court that will ultimately have to test the validity of the legal or ritual system that brought the adoption into being.

The different types of adoption can be defined as follows.

Foreign

A foreign adoption is an adoption ordered in a legal jurisdiction outside England and Wales, be it from a designated country or not. Adoption orders made in Scotland, Northern Ireland, the Isle of Man and the Channel Islands are foreign adoption orders from designated countries and are automaticaly recognised without recourse to adoptive proceedings in England and Wales.

Overseas

An overseas adoption is a foreign adoption that comes within the terms of the Adoption Act 1976, s.72(2), namely, "an adoption of such a description as the Secretary of State may by order specify, being a description of adoptions of children appearing to him to be effected under the law of any country outside Great Britain; and an order under this subsection may contain provision as to the manner in which evidence of an overseas adoption may be given." The specification of overseas adoptions was made by the Adoption (Designation of Overseas Adoptions) Order 1973 and relates to adoptions made by statute in any of 39 Commonwealth countries and United Kingdom dependent territories or 22 other countries named in the Schedule, all of which are designated countries whose adoption orders will be automatically recognised as if they had been made by an English court (section

38(1)(d)). The child must not have reached the age of 18 and have not been married. (For further information, see Chap. 5). Recourse to court will not be necessary if the Secretary of State has granted entry and citizenship.

Convention

A Convention adoption is an adoption granted in a country which has ratified the Hague Convention on Jurisdiction, Applicable Law and Recognition of Decrees relating to Adoption 1965. The Adoption Act 1976, s.17 ratified the 1965 Convention in the United Kingdom. The Convention has only been ratified by the United Kingdom, Austria and Switzerland. The Adoption Rules 1984 apply to a Convention adoption. Convention adoptions will require recourse to an adoption application in England and Wales.

The term Convention adoption can also refer to adoptions from countries who are signatories of the Hague Convention on Intercountry Adoption 1993 (listed in App. 1D). Whilst England and Wales is such a signatory, the 1993 Convention has not as yet been incorporated into our law. A new Adoption Act is expected to do this (see Chap. 14).

Inter-country

International adoptions by their very nature will be inter-country, but the term tends to refer to adoptions between countries where agreements exist. The Hague Convention on Inter-Country Adoption 1993 will ensure that there is a recognised procedure for adopting children in one country and then removing them to another without the duplication of an adoption application.

In the case of a foreign child abandoned in England and Wales, for example, such a child's consideration for adoption will have an international element, by reason of his nationality, but it will not be regularised inter-country *per se* because the child was not formally adopted elsewhere before being brought to England and Wales. So inter-country, as far as that child is concerned, would not really describe the adoption process.

Designated

An adoption from a designated country will be automatically recognised in England and Wales as the order derives from an accepted legal system for ordering adoptions, but recourse to court is still probably necessary, despite the recognition depending upon the attitude of the Secretary of State.

It might well be that a declaration as opposed to an adoption application will be sufficient for the court of England and Wales to grant the necessary recognition of the adoption.

Non-designated

An adoption from a non-designated country will not be automatically recognised in England and Wales as the order derives from a country that does not have an acceptable legal system for ordering adoptions. An application in a court in England and Wales must take place.

Common Law

The common law may recognise an adoption under the law of a country outside England and Wales, even though it is likely to have been made under the common or customary law of that country rather than under statute. Both of the applicants and the child must have been domiciled in the country where the order was made. Even if only one of the applicants was so domiciled, it is possible that the order will be recognised in England and Wales under the common law. But a domestic application will have to be made to clarify this.

Legal

A legal adoption is an adoption from a country whose legal system is recognised in England and Wales.

De facto

A *de facto* adoption refers to an adoption that has taken place in a country that has no legal adoptive process, but where there has been a genuine transfer of responsibility between the natural parents of the child and the applicants. In such circumstances, a court of England and Wales is likely to consider the adoption as having taken place *de facto*. Such adoptions will not be recognised automatically in England and Wales, so there will have to be a domestic adoption application as well.

Agency

Agency adoptions are adoptions granted outside a legal system, by an adoption agency recognised within its own country as having the capacity to arrange for the adoption of children by properly vetted applicants. Whilst outside of legal authorisation, such agency adoptions are likely to have a structure and an attitude that is recognised as being effective. Agency adoptions will not automatically be recognised within England and Wales and fresh proceedings will have to take place as such an agency adoption order, where it exists, will have derived from a non-designated country.

Family

A family adoption is an adoption by a relative or friend of the child or his family. Such adoptions are not uncommon in India, for example, but

7

for immigration purposes will not be accepted by an entry clearance officer or an immigration officer in England or Wales. The country is not likely to be a designated country and recourse to court for a domestic application will be essential. However, the court will consider the full background of what happened in the country where the family adoption took place, in order to consider whether it was genuine or fraudulent, before granting a domestic adoption order.

Private

Private adoptions are adoptions arranged privately by applicants travelling abroad outside of any recognised legal system, but possibly within the framework of a recognised foreign adoption agency. As the country is unlikely to be a designated country, there will be no automatic recognition in England and Wales and recourse to court for a domestic application will be essential.

Embassy

While Embassy adoptions *per se* are probably non-existent nowadays, there is evidence of adoptions taking place abroad via embassies, in terms of formal or informal contacts that a consular office or Embassy has locally. The Embassy may have contacts with orphanages or may understand the legal requirements of the country in which it is situated and as such may appear to act as an adoption agency. If such adoptions do occur, a domestic application in this country will have to take place.

Chapter 2

BRINGING A CHILD INTO ENGLAND AND WALES

The following procedure applies regardless of whether the child is being brought into England and Wales from a designated or a non-designated country because the immigration authorities and the family courts still need clarification of the removal to and entry into England and Wales from whatever country.

Initial Steps

The applicants should first contact their local authority and tell them of their plans to adopt a child from abroad. This should be done before attempts are made to bring a child into the country. The local authority needs advance notice of an intention to adopt from abroad in order to commence and complete their homestudy assessment report regarding the suitability of the applicants as parents. (For details of the duties of the local authority, see Chap. 7.)

The homestudy assessment report is not the same as the report under Schedule 2 of the Adoption Rules 1984. The latter is still required, but later on in the adoption process as it is a requirement of the domestic process and not the international process. Whatever order there might be regarding the child from the sending country, at present he will still need an adoption order or declaration of the English Court. A Schedule 2 report will need to be completed as a statutory requirement of making a domestic adoption application.

The homestudy assessment report is likely to deal with the following:

(a) suitability of applicants in terms of age, capability and commitment, as with any domestic application.
(b) suitability of accommodation.
(c) an ability to reasonably maintain the child.

Theoretically, the requirements of applicants for an international adoption are the same as for ordinary domestic adoption though it has been said that the requirements are stricter, regarding capability for example. The local authority will want to be very certain of the applicants' suitability before commencing the difficult process for the child, of coming into England and Wales from the sending country. Health and age is known to have been a reason for refusal in the past, though any local authority will have to properly support their reasons for a rejection in case they face judicial review of that refusal.

If the child has already been located abroad then as much information as possible should be made available to the local authority, such as:

(a) age, sex and address of the child.

(b) consent and identify of natural parents where they are known.

(c) consent and identify of orphanage, if the child is an orphan, and whether such an orphanage is recognised by the sending country.

(d) if the applicants have already obtained an adoption order in the sending country, details of the adoption.

(e) if the Home Office and Department of Health are already aware of the identity of the child and applications for entry clearance, all details regarding those.

(f) if the sending country has made a preliminary consideration of the applicants but has not made a final order because awaiting the local authority homestudy assessment report, then any directions of the foreign court should be communicated.

Where documentation is in a foreign language, the local authority and Home Office will require translations. It will be for the applicants to both fund and provide these. Certain sending countries and certain English Consular Offices have addresses of State translators.

The local authority will evaluate all information received from the sending country and give its recommendation to the Department of Health in England, or the Welsh Office in Wales (see App. 7, for addresses). It must be stressed that the assessment report deals with the suitability of the applicants; it will be the Schedule 2 report that deals with the suitability of the match between applicants and child.

The Department of Health or the Welsh Office will then advise the Home Office. Where there has been a positive recommendation, entry clearance will in due course be given as long as immigration requirements have been fulfilled regarding the child (see Chap. 8, below). The Home Office will advise the Foreign and Commonwealth Office.

Where a child has already been located in a particular sending country, the Foreign and Commonwealth Office will advise the entry clearance officer at the British Embassy or Consular Office, if the applicants have not done so themselves. If and when the adoption order is made in the sending country, and if and when permission for the child to leave is granted, such papers will be sent to the British Embassy and entry clearance will be granted as long as the immigration requirements are fulfilled regarding the child.

Where a child or country has not been located at the time of the positive recommendation, the applicants should advise the British Embassy or Consular Office as soon as they have located a child. The court of the sending country will learn that there is already a positive local authority recommendation but is likely to want to know if entry clearance into England and Wales will be granted, so that a child is not left in a state of limbo, before either making an adoption order or stating that the child is permitted to leave the country.

Procedure Abroad

Where a child has not already been located the applicants can seek the help of various adoption agencies in England and abroad (see App. 7 for useful addresses) or contact British Embassies, who might have information to assist in locating children or orphanages and may be able to advise upon the usual legal procedure of the particular country.

Some countries will want the child to be adopted by the applicants under their legal system before departure, others might not formally have the child adopted but simply grant leave for the applicants to remove the child. Some will want prior clarification regarding a positive homestudy assessment report and entry clearance into England and Wales, others are more lax.

Where a British Embassy or adoption agency cannot ultimately assist then the applicants must make their own arrangements, contacting any national or local bureaux, for example, in the foreign country. Only the High Court can authorise the making of arrangements to adopt a child by a person other than a recognised adoption agency: *Re A (Adoption: Placement)* [1988] 1 W.L.R. 229 (see further, App. 5).

Some courts abroad require the child to stay temporarily in England and Wales with the applicants before making a final adoption or removal order. Entry clearance will still be required from the British Embassy who must be advised of the child's temporary stay for the purpose of further clarification of the assessment.

When an order is made by the foreign court and entry clearance is granted the child will travel on his own passport granted by the entry clearance officer or on the passport of one of the applicants that has been duly stamped to that effect.

As 12 months must elapse before the applicants can obtain their domestic adoption or seek a declaration in the courts of England and Wales, the child is likely to be granted about 12 months limited leave to remain in England and Wales. An application or declaration can be sought before the end of 12 months but 12 months must elapse before an order or declaration is obtained.

Upon Return to England and Wales

The applicants must notify the local authority as soon as they return with the child. The local authority will then commence the Schedule 2 report.

At the expiry of 12 months the applicants can regulate their position regarding the child and seek an adoption order. If the child comes from Austria or Switzerland then the applicants will be making a Convention application (see Chap. 6); otherwise they will be seeking an ordinary domestic adoption order (see Chap. 4).

Chapter 3

OBTAINING ADOPTION ORDERS ABROAD

This book is not intended to deal specifically with the procedure for obtaining adoption orders in jurisdictions outside England and Wales. However, some general advice can be given.

Attitudes to Adoption in Other Countries

Applicants must bear in mind certain aspects of foreign legal systems and associated attitudes regarding the adoption of children by foreigners, who then remove those children to their own country. Some countries are content with such applications and have a structure for dealing with them. Others are less happy. The country's culture often determines this attitude and applicants should make themselves aware of it.

Embassies or Consular offices around the United Kingdom can be contacted by applicants to ascertain the attitude and demands of foreign countries regarding inter-country adoption. Embassies may be able to put the applicants in touch with the legal body which deals with such applications in their country, if they are aware of its existence and location.

Some foreign countries are perhaps not as willing as they once were to allow their children to be either adopted then taken out of the country or removed to be adopted in England and Wales. Some foreign legal systems may not entertain an application for adoption from applicants from England and Wales until they have seen evidence of the suitability of the applicants themselves from the Department of Health.

Even designated countries may still seek clarification of the position of the applicants in England and Wales prior to making an adoption order or allowing a child to be removed for adoption.

Information Required About the Applicants

Evidence sought from the Department of Health will be in the form of documentation comprising a home study report from the local authority (see Chap. 7 for the content of this report). It is for this reason that the applicants should notify their local authority of their intentions prior to making their application abroad. If the applicants have not, they run the risk of the foreign country sending them back to obtain the home study assessment, before their application will be entertained.

Once completed, the home study report should be sent by the local authority either directly to the appropriate authority, legal representative or agency abroad, or through the Department of Health if they have had any involvement.

The agency abroad will want to receive as much information as the local authority can provide. Such information should deal with all aspects of the applicants' suitability in terms of accommodation, health and police checks. Certain agencies abroad will be aware that local authorities are expected to provide their own home study reports and in those circumstances any private home study reports commissioned by the applicants and relied upon by a local authority could be rejected. Adept agencies will want to see a Department of Health certification that proves that the home study has been carried out by an approved adoption agency.

The Procedure Abroad

Applicants should realise that the jurisdictions in which they will make the adoption applications are foreign to the legal jurisdiction of England and Wales. They should be aware that the legal requirements of those jurisdictions can change with little or no advance notice. Research should therefore be done to ensure applications meet those requirements, which may even change in the course of making the application.

Certain countries expect the applicants to have nominated a notary or lawyer abroad to represent them regarding their application. Their respective agencies are also likely to expect that the name and address of such a notary be advanced to the adoption agency prior to making the application. The Department of Health is likely to correspond with the applicants asking them to nominate the notary so that all papers can be sent to the notary's office before the adoption application comes to the foreign court for a hearing.

The Department of Health, when it is directly involved, is responsible for sending the papers to the Embassy or Consulate and the Notary abroad, where one is required and has been nominated. The Department of Health might also be asked to send the papers directly to the adoption agency abroad, where such an agency, as is likely, exists.

Some countries may nominate a particular child, or even two or three, from which the applicants can make their choice. Sometimes an orphanage itself is nominated so that the applicants can go and see for themselves. Once more, the manner in which a choice is made can vary from country to country.

Some countries will not allow the applicants to apply for an adoption order, but for a transfer of parental responsibility instead. This can cause legal complications later on if the country is not a designated country, as well as causing problems when seeking entry clearance into England and Wales.

Probationary Periods

Some countries make adoption orders that are not final until the satisfactory completion of a probationary period. These systems demand approval in advance of their own adoption order and of the placement in England and Wales.

Some countries may be satisfied with the home study report as far as it assesses the parents, but might require the child to go temporarily to England and Wales for a final assessment to be carried out, and only grant the adoption order if satisfied with the contents of the final assessment local authority home study report. England and Wales is likely to grant temporary leave to remain for a child entering the country in those temporary circumstances through the entry clearance officer, but a foreign adoption order made once and for all prior to the child entering England and Wales is obviously going to be preferred for immigration and other legal purposes.

Where a child does come to England and Wales temporarily, then before the final assessment is received by the foreign country, they may require monthly bulletins of the child's progress.

Chapter 4

THE ADOPTION PROCEDURE IN ENGLAND AND WALES

This chapter documents the adoption procedure in England and Wales where an adoption order has been obtained abroad from a non-Convention country. The adoption procedure recorded here is one where the applicants notified the local authority before applying for the adoption order abroad so that a home study assessment report on the applicants has already been prepared, prior either to the adoption abroad or to entry clearance being granted. The same procedure will be followed where the applicants did not notify the local authority, but it is unlikely to be as smooth under those circumstances.

For the procedure regarding the recognition in England and Wales of an Overseas adoption or a Convention adoption, see Chapters 5 and 6 respectively.

The Adoption Act 1976

The Adoption Act 1976 is the statute under which children are adopted in the United Kingdom. The procedure for a child already adopted in a foreign country whose adoption orders are not recognised in England and Wales is the same as for a domestic application. Whilst that procedure is easily found in any book dealing with domestic adoption, the main considerations are recorded here.

Principally, the court and the local authority must have regard to all the circumstances of the case and must safeguard and promote the welfare of the child throughout his childhood (s.6).

The adoption order must not be made unless the court is satisfied that sufficient opportunities have been taken for the child to be seen with the applicants at home by the local authority (s.13(3)). It is primarily for this reason that entry clearance must be given by the entry clearance officer. If entry clearance is not permitted, no opportunity will be afforded for the requirement that the local authority see the child with the applicants to be fulfilled.

Domicile and Marital Status

Where the applicants are married, at least one of them must be domiciled in part of the United Kingdom, the Channel Islands or the Isle of Man. For the purpose of an adoption in the United Kingdom, as opposed to just England and Wales, one of the applicants must be resident in England, Northern Ireland, Scotland or Wales.

A single person making an adoption application must have attained the age of 21 and must be domiciled and resident in the United Kingdom, the Channel Islands or the Isle of Man. Under section 15(1)(a) of the Adoption Act, he can either be unmarried, or if married, the court must be satisfied that:

(i) the spouse cannot be found; or

(ii) the spouse is living apart from the applicant and the separation is likely to be permanent; or

(iii) the spouse, by reason of ill-health, whether physical or mental, is incapable of making an application for an adoption order.

It ought to be borne in mind that it could be particularly difficult for a single person to adopt a child from abroad. That is not to say that it will be impossible, but because the court will be particularly careful in its deliberations on whether to allow a foreign child to reside here by reason of an adoption order, the single applicant will have to convince the court that the commitment offered by him is in the child's interest.

Preliminary Procedure

The matter will usually be set down in the county court: see *Practice Direction (Adoption: Transfer of Proceedings)* in Appendix 5, below. Problematic cases can then be sent up to the High Court or even set down in the High Court at first instance.

The first step is to file an originating application in the local county court. The local authority will be the respondent to the proceedings by virtue of rule 15(2) of the Adoption Rules 1984, as under section 22 of the Adoption Act 1976 they will have been given notice of the intention to apply for an adoption order by the applicants when the child first entered the country. In any case, they would have issued the home study report on the applicants prior to the child's entry and so would have knowledge of the applicants prior to the making of the domestic application.

Necessary directions will be given prior to the main hearing.

1. *Documents*

The court will require three copies of the following:

(i) the originating summons application;

(ii) all information relied upon when the adoption was made in the court abroad;

(iii) all documents translated into English with a certificate authorising their translation;

(iv) the agreement of the natural parents or the dispensation from consent;

(v) the affidavit of the applicants setting out the entire background of the case;

(vi) the affidavit of the local authority social worker detailing their entire involvement;

(vii) the homestudy assessment report;

(viii) the local authority Schedule 2 report as to the suitability of the placement, covering all of the requirements set out in the Adoption Rules 1984, r.22(1) lodged by the local authority.

2. *Dispensation from Parental Consent*

If the child's parents cannot be found, the court can dispense with parental consent to the adoption, even if it is not known for sure whether they had consciously abandoned their child: *Re R (Adoption)* [1967] 1 W.L.R. 34 (see App. 5). Similarly, where a parent has done nothing to discharge his parental obligations to the child, his consent to the adoption can be dispensed with; *Re B (S) (An Infant)* [1968] Ch. 204 (see App. 5).

The Role of the Local Authority

The local authority will have provided the initial homestudy assessment report, as well as its separate Schedule 2 report.

As with any ordinary domestic adoption, the application will have gone before the Adoption Panel, in compliance with the Adoption Panel Regulations 1983, for its approval. Though this will have been considered by the local authority when preparing the schedule and report.

The Role of the Guardian or Official Solicitor

The child will be represented in the county court by the 'Guardian *ad litem.* The Guardian must consider all matters in the applicants' originating process, affidavit, local authority Schedule 2 report and homestudy report that may have been relied upon before the child was adopted abroad and before the child entered England and Wales.

The Guardian must advise whether the child should be present at the hearing and should consider anything that he believes the court will need clarification on. The Guardian can furnish an interim report if the court deems that necessary.

The Guardian's report is confidential and the applicants have no automatic right to see it. However, when the Guardian's and local authority's reports have been filed, the court can give directions as to whether they should be disclosed prior to the hearing. Under rule 53(2) of the Adoption Rules, the court can impose conditions on what can be revealed. It is likely that the applicants will be aware of much of the local authority report in any event, by reason of the fact that it formed part of the adoption hearing abroad.

As the foreign adoption papers will already have been seen by the parties, including the papers dealing with the natural parents' consent or dispensation with consent, the Guardian's task in meeting the requirements of the Adoption Act will be easier.

Much of the background in terms of the applicants' suitability will have been clarified in advance of the adoption abroad, and the domestic court will not necessarily want to duplicate matters that are corroborated in documentary form from that hearing. The Guardian and local authority can rely upon it to confirm aspects of the placement that they might ordinarily have gone into.

The courts of England and Wales will, however, want to be satisfied that once the child is living with the applicants, both the local authority and the Guardian think that the placement is good.

The Official Solicitor in the High Court will have a similar role to the Guardian or simply as *amicus curiae*. If the case is transferred to the High Court is likely to be retained.

The Hearing

The following persons should attend:

(i) a social worker employed by the relevant local authority;

(ii) the child (unless the court has already directed otherwise under rule 23(5));

(iii) the Guardian, unless directed otherwise;

(iv) the applicants.

Under rule 23(3) the proceedings should be conducted with a view to ensuring that the applicants are not seen or made known to any respondent not already aware of the applicants' identify. For international adoption purposes this is probably academic as the consent of the natural parents abroad has either been obtained or dispensed with already.

Considerations of the Court

Even though a foreign adoption order has been made, for domestic purposes the requirements of the Adoption Act 1976 must still be met. Therefore, the court must be satisfied that:

(i) the child is free for adoption;

(ii) every person whose consent is required has freely agreed, unconditionally and with understanding;

(iii) the parents' consent has been obtained or dispensed with;

(iv) every person who can be found and whose consent to the order's making is needed has received notice of the date and place of the hearing;

(v) no offences were committed regarding the obtaining of the child for adoption.

Factual considerations that the court will take into account in reaching its decision are:

(i) the need to safeguard and promote the welfare of the child throughout his childhood;

(ii) the wishes and feelings of the child;

(iii) the age and understanding of the child;

(iv) the religious upbringing and ethnic background of the child.

The court can decide whether terms and conditions should be imposed upon the adoption order (such as contact with the natural parents) or whether a residence order with parental responsibility under section 8 of the Children Act 1989 might be preferable to an adoption order.

The Adoption Order

If granted, the adoption order should be served within seven days upon the following, by virtue of section 52(4) of the Adoption Act 1976:

(i) the applicants;

(ii) the registrar general, who is responsible for maintaining an adoption register (Adoption Act 1976, s.50);

(iii) every respondent to the proceedings;

(iv) any other court that has already been appraised of an aspect of the child's life;

(v) any other person, with leave.

Citizenship

Once an adoption order is obtained it should be sent to the Home Office with the child's passport for a British passport to be issued. If the applicants are British, the child will automatically become a British citizen (British Nationality Act 1981).

Where the applicants are not British citizens, but have permanent residence on the day of the adoption order, the child will follow his new parents' immigration status and become a naturalised citizen when they do so.

If a child is adopted abroad and there is, unusually, no application before the English court for recognition of that adoption, then citizenship is at the discretion of the Home Secretary.

A child born in the United Kingdom to parents who are settled and ordinarily resident, but are not British citizens, will be a British citizen irrespective of whether he is adopted by British citizens in due course (British Nationality Act 1981, s.1(1)).

The Home Office can strip applicants of citizenship obtained through registration or naturalisation, where,

(i) it was obtained by fraud or by misrepresentation of some material fact; or

(ii) where an offence involving disloyalty to the Crown or trading unlawfully with an enemy country in time of war has been committed; or

(iii) the applicant is sentenced to a period of more than 12 months' imprisonment during the five years following the date of registration or naturalisation.

This can affect the citizenship of the applicants' child. However, if the child has been adopted in England, it is unlikely that the applicants will be stripped of their citizenship if this would affect the stability of the child.

Chapter 5

OVERSEAS ADOPTIONS

Generally

Overseas adoption orders are those made under the law of a country outside of Great Britain which is specified in the Schedule to the Adoption (Designation of Overseas Adoptions) Order 1973, namely any of the 39 Commonwealth countries and United Kingdom Dependent Territories, and 22 other countries which have been specified by Order in Council (see App. 2G).

Such adoptions must have been made under statute and the interested child cannot have reached the age of 18 or have been married. Citizenship is not automatic in respect of these overseas adoption orders, even though they are recognised in England and Wales

Where such an order has been made abroad, a certified copy of the order or a certificate signed by someone having legal authority to do so stating that the adoption has been effected, must be given to the nearest consular office. These documents will be forwarded to the Home Office to facilitate entry clearance.

Recognition of the Adoption

Where an adoption is specified as an "overseas adoption", it can be said to be already recognised under section 38(1) (d) of the Adoption Act 1976. However, for the avoidance of doubt, it may be better to seek a declaration that the adoption is valid.

Under the Family Proceedings Rules 1991, rr.3.15 (see App. 2F) and 3.16, an application can be made to the High Court for a declaration that the applicant is the adopted child of a specified person in accordance with the Adoption Act 1976, s.39 (see App. 3E). The applicant will be the adopted child, who by reason of the fact that he is a minor, can make the application through the adoptive parent as next-friend.

The applicant has to be domiciled in England and Wales at the date of the application for a declaration, or must have been habitually resident in England and Wales throughout the previous year. Therefore, if the child is seeking the declaration himself or through a next-friend, he will need to have resided in England and Wales for 12 months prior to the application being made.

Procedure for Obtaining a Declaration

(i) An originating application must be drawn up.

(ii) This should have an accompanying affidavit stating how the order came to be made, by which court and in what circumstances and exhibiting as much documentary evidence surrounding the original application and order as is available.

(iii) All documents generated abroad where the language is not English must be provided in translation.

1. *The Court's Approach*

The court will probably only make the declaration sought where the documentation required for a domestic adoption application accompanies the application for a declaration. Thus the court will want to be satisfied that the natural parents' consent was obtained, that a proper procedure was carried out in removing the child legally from abroad and that the local authority approve. Indeed, it is likely that all the requirements for a domestic adoption under the Adoption Act 1976 will have to be met, as to which see Chapter 4.

Where there is any doubt as to those requirements being met, the court is unlikely to make the declaration. An ordinary adoption application with all the necessary documentary evidence in support will then have to be made.

Under section 53(2) (a) of the Adoption Act, the court can refuse to make the declaration, or recognise the adoption order at all, by reason of the fact that the authority which authorised the adoption was not a competent authority.

For the effect of a declaration on citizenship, see Chapter 4.

2. *Registration*

When a declaration has been made, notification must be given to the Adopted Children Register, General Register Office (Adoption Act 1976, s.50).

Chapter 6

CONVENTION ADOPTIONS

Generally

A Convention adoption is an adoption order made in accordance with section 17(1) of the Adoption Act 1976. The convention referred to is the Hague Convention on Adoption 1965, which the United Kingdom ratified in 1978 (see App. 1B).

The countries who have ratified the convention are the United Kingdom, Switzerland and Austria. Adoptions that are ordered in one country which has ratified the 1965 Convention are enforceable in any other. The court can make a convention adoption order where the prospective adoptive parents or the child are related through nationality or habitual residence to another convention country (Adoption Act 1976, s.17).

Although the 1965 Convention is now part of English law, because only two other countries have ratified it, it is not in reality a particularly important piece of legislation. Indeed, recourse to a domestic application is still likely to take place, as the procedure below indicates.

The Child

The child, who has already been adopted in a Convention country, must:

(i) be a national of or habitually resident in a Convention country; and

(ii) not be or ever have been married; and

(iii) be under the age of 18.

Where the child is not a national of England and Wales, the order should not be made unless the court is satisfied that each person who gave their agreement to the adoption did so in accordance with any internal law of the relevant foreign country and with full understanding of what was involved.

Procedure

The Adoption Rules 1984, Pts. I, III and V apply. The procedure under those rules is as follows.

(i) An originating summons in Form 6 must be filed in the county court, stating that the application is for a Convention adoption (see App. 3A).

(ii) The applicants should state their nationality and residency and that of the child.

(iii) All documents that might have been relied upon in the convention country where the child was adopted should be exhibited.

(iv) There must be a statement by an expert in the law of that country as to the nationality of the applicants and child, if not citizens of the United Kingdom, and as to those provisions of the internal law of that country which relate to an agreement to an adoption abroad. The expert will have to swear an affidavit regarding the internal law, giving evidence of those qualifications which permit him to be classed as an expert.

(v) If the child is a national of England and Wales, the requirements of section 16 of the Adoption Act 1976 relating to parental consent must be met.

(vi) Any document showing the agreement of the natural parents to the adoption must comply with the internal law of the Convention country.

(vii) If the document showing the agreement of the natural parents is witnessed, there need not be evidence that the signature of the parents is valid. If not, such evidence will be necessary.

(viii) If the court is dissatisfied with the evidence of consent it can adjourn the application for further evidence to be submitted.

The Role of the Local Authority

Technically, it should be possible to seek a declaration in recognition of a convention adoption without local authority involvement. However, the domestic court will probably want clarification of the suitability of the placement before making the declaration.

The local authority has the same duty to the court in relation to an adoption from a convention country as for any foreign adoption. For those duties, see Chapter 7.

If the applicants have not advised their local authority before applying to the Convention country for the adoption and, unlikely though it is, they have been able to bring the child into the United Kingdom and seek to have him adopted without a local authority homestudy assessment report first being made, the local authority will have to completely assess the parents before going on to assess the placement of the child with them.

The Role of the Guardian or Official Solicitor

See Chapter 4.

Considerations of the Court

If the applicants are both nationals of the same Convention country, the court cannot make an order if the internal law of that country prohibits the order being made in this country (Adoption Act 1976, s.17(4)).

The order will probably be made once the following have been satisfied.

(i) If the child is not a United Kingdom national, the requirements of the internal law of the relevant Convention country on adoption relating to consent and consultations have been met (Adoption Act 1976, s.17(6)).

(ii) The consent of the natural parents, or parties having parental responsibility for the child, has been given according to the internal law of the relevant Convention country.

(iii) The local authority has agreed.

(iv) The Guardian *ad litem* has agreed.

Notification of the Order

The following should be notified within seven days of an order being made.

(i) The Registrar General.

(ii) The equivalent body of the Convention country of which the child is a national.

(iii) The equivalent body of the country where the child was born, if different.

(iv) The equivalent body of the country where the applicants habitually reside.

(v) If one of the applicants is not a United Kingdom national, the equivalent body of his home country.

Citizenship

See Chapter 4.

International Recognition

A Convention adoption is regarded in the same way as an overseas adoption and will be recognised in other countries who have ratified the Convention (Adoption Act 1976, s.53(2)).

Chapter 7

LOCAL AUTHORITY DUTIES

When the Child is to be Brought to England and Wales

1. *The Role of the Local Authority*

A local authority is expected to assess, counsel and prepare applicants before a child is identified for possible adoption, or provisionally placed, whether the adoption application will be to a designated or non-designated country. When the Hague Convention on Intercountry Adoption 1993 becomes law, as the government intends, the local authority will be obliged by statute to arrange for all assessments, whereas the present requirement is non-statutory.

The local authority makes its assessment on the basis that the application will be through a properly authorised overseas agency or statutory authority that operates proper safeguards and controls and that will not release a child until the requirements of both countries have been met. It is up to the applicants to provide the local authority with proof of the status of the overseas adoption agency.

2. *The Assessment*

The local authority assessment should take the form of a homestudy report. The same thoroughness and standards are to be applied as apply in the case of those seeking to adopt a British child; superficial investigations and assessments at lower standards are not acceptable. A person who cannot be recommended as an adopter of a British child cannot be recommended to adopt a foreign child.

Reports are asked to be provided as quickly as is possible, and no more than six months should elapse for preparation, counselling and assessment to be completed including the recommendation to the Department of Health. However, if a particular local authority has a large number of applicants making applications for an overseas adoption the timescale will be accepted as being longer.

Where applicants have already been approved by an adoption agency the procedure might be quicker. If no adoption agency has approved the applicants, the local authority's adoption panel can consider the applicants just as if the application were for a British child, but their role is solely advisory and consultative on the international plain.

Reports when completed should not be given to the applicants, although every aspect of the procedure should be consistently discussed with them.

Full police checks and a health report on the applicants will be expected to form a part of the assessment. Each application should be considered individually and the age of the applicants must be considered objectively. The homestudy report must examine the understanding of the applicants, their ability to foresee difficult events in the child's life, the ability to cope with practical and emotional problems, the awareness of trans-culture.

The placement of one child alone is preferred, but consideration of siblings should be given if sought. Both applicants should meet the child before he comes to England and Wales and counselling must be given from an approved agency, as required by the Adoption Act 1976.

Privately commissioned homestudy reports can be considered to be in breach of sections 11, 57 and 72(3) of the Adoption Act 1976. Furthermore, homestudy reports for adoptions in England and Wales should not be converted into homestudy reports for adoptions abroad. Privately commissioned reports cannot be endorsed or validated by the local authority. However, if a further homestudy report is required for entry clearance purposes, a report by an approved adoption agency will be sufficient.

The local authority should recommend whether the Department of Health should give certification for the adoption taking place.

The local authority can charge for the homestudy report, though if they simply have to bring a report up to date they ought to make no further charge.

3. *After the Arrival of the Child*

Applicants ought to advise the local authority as soon as a child enters England and Wales. In case this does not happen, the local authority should periodically check upon the applicants as to whether entry has occurred. When the child has arrived, the local authority should expect to receive an application for adoption before the court from the applicants if the country is non-designated.

Where the child's country of origin is designated, the applicants might still seek a declaration in the High Court that their overseas adoption is valid in England and Wales and the local authority will be expected to intervene.

If the adoption agency abroad has required the child to stay temporarily in England and Wales prior to making its final order, the local authority must provide a final assessment and, if sought by the foreign court, a month-by-month assessment in the meantime. Until a child is adopted under the law of his country of origin, *i.e.* while in England and Wales for a probationary period, he will have the status of a child accommodated by the local authority.

When the Child is to be Removed from England and Wales

In respect of applications to remove a child from England and Wales for adoption abroad under Schedule 2, para. 19 of the Children Act 1989 (see App. 2C) the local authority can arrange and help in arranging for a child in its care to live outside England and Wales with the court's agreement. This might take the form of communicating with a local authority abroad where the child will reside or a report to assist the court and/or local authority abroad.

When the Child has been Abandoned

If a child is abandoned, whether by prospective adopters, foreign nationals or immigrants with insecure status, the local authority where the child last resided is responsible for the child and must accommodate him or receive him into care.

If such a child had been subject to an international adoption application and such an application has fallen through for whatever reason the local authority should contact the country of origin, either by itself or with the assistance of the Department of Health and the Home Office to consider returning the child.

There is no procedure for forcing a country to receive back a child and it is unlikely that any country would deport a child in such circumstances. If there is a wish to receive back the child, the local authority should refer the matter to the court for its decision upon the child's future. If the local authority does not believe it is in the interest of the child to be returned for whatever reason, the court should be so advised. However, the local authority will probably wish to relieve itself of its legal obligation and return the child to its own country and culture.

If it is established that the child has indeed been abandoned, then that child, whether accommodated or in care, will be looked upon in the same way as any other child in care, whom the local authority can consider placing for adoption. A local authority adoption panel will be able to consider finding a suitable adoptive family in this country for the child.

Chapter 8

IMMIGRATION PROCEDURE

The following aspects of immigration procedure must be borne in mind when seeking to adopt a child from abroad. The procedure derives from the Immigration Act 1981 and Home Office Circulars.

Generally

No child can enter the United Kingdom without permission being granted for him to do so by the Home Office.

Rule 50 of the Immigration Rules 1983, states that adopted children under the age of 18, provided they are unmarried, are to be admitted for settlement. The statement of Changes in the Immigration Rules (1994) (H.C. 395), para. 310, emphasises that a child of an adoptive parent cannot enter unless there has been a genuine transfer of parental responsibility on the ground of the birth parents' inability to look after the child and the adoption is not one of convenience arranged to facilitate the child's admission.

If one parent, or a relative other than a parent, is settled in the United Kingdom and there are serious and compelling family or other considerations which make exclusion undesirable, for example where the other parent is physically or mentally incapable of looking after the child, and suitable arrangements have been made for the child's care, then the child will be allowed entry.

Home Office Considerations

There is no Directive in the Immigration Rules for a foreign child to enter the United Kingdom for the purposes of adoption. The Home Secretary will at times use his discretion to allow entry, if he is satisfied that it is in the interests of the child in all the circumstances of the case.

In the case of an inter-country adoption from a non-designated country, an application will have to be made here for a domestic adoption order even when the child has already been adopted abroad (see Chap. 4). Before that can be done, the Home Office has to consider whether the applicants and the child they wish to adopt fulfil the requirements of the Immigration Rules relating to the admission of children for settlement.

The Role of the Department of Health

As stated above, the Home Office will have to be satisfied that the proposed adoption involves the genuine transfer of parental responsibility. While considering the merits of the application, the Home Office will advise the Department of Health of the applications for entry clearance and for a domestic adoption (unless it was notified by the applicants before the foreign adoption took place). The Department of Health will then instruct the local authority to carry out its assessment report on the prospective adopters, where this has not already been done. If no report exists, the local authority may seek the applicants' return to England without the child for an assessment of their capability as prospective adoptive parents to be completed.

Sometimes applicants obtain the foreign adoption order and return home for the assessment without trying to gain entry clearance first. It is, of course, preferable if they have ensured that the local authority assessment is completed as far as possible prior to their adoption application abroad, and have sought entry clearance for the child before arriving at the port of entry.

If the Department of Health is satisfied with the local authority assessment report, it will inform the Home Office which is then unlikely to refuse entry clearance for a limited period of time prior to the domestic adoption order being made. Entry clearance will be granted for a minimum of 12 months, as the child and the applicants must live together in England for at least that period before a domestic adoption order can be made.

The Application for Entry Clearance

As only the domestic court can decide whether the child should be adopted by the applicants in this country, entry clearance must be obtained to allow the local authority to complete its assessment where it has already begun one and to allow the English court to make its final decision.

As soon as the applicants have pinpointed either a specific child or the country from which they wish to adopt, they should contact the local British Embassy or Consulate. This may be able to grant entry clearance itself if it has its own entry clearance officer. If the embassy or consular address abroad is unknown, applicants should write to the Migration and Visa Department, Foreign and Commonwealth Office. They have a list of all British diplomatic posts abroad.

An application for entry clearance can be made by the applicants themselves or someone else acting on behalf of the child. In the latter case a certified letter must be shown, proving that authority exists to act for the applicants.

The application can be made in person or by post; fax is not acceptable. Certain consular posts require an interview first. If the Consular post does not have an entry clearance officer, the application cannot be made in person.

1. *Documentation*

The applicants must provide:

(i) a letter stating why entry clearance is required;

(ii) a completed adoption questionnaire if given one (see App. 4A);

(iii) a medical report on the child (see App. 4B);

(iv) the reasons for the adoption;

(v) details of the child's parentage and history;

(vi) proof of the consent of the natural parents;

(vii) an orphanage report, if the child is an orphan;

(viii) certification of the child's abandonment, if he was abandoned;

(ix) the location of the child's permanent home;

(x) all court papers that are available, translated into English;

(xi) any social inquiry report relied upon by the foreign court;

(xii) the fee for the Home Office (in the region of £100).

As many documents should be in the English language as is possible and original documents should be included. Where originals are lacking, a certificate of authenticity of a copy should be included where possible. Ultimately, it will be a matter for the Home Office to accept the documents or not. The Home Office can also demand that all documents be in English.

If the foreign parents were married, both their consents are required, and they have to have been given freely. If they were unmarried, only the mother's consent is required. If there is a lack of detail about consent, this could cause problems in the domestic application for adoption in England and Wales because parental consent must be shown to have been properly given.

The staff of the diplomatic post will check that all the documents are in order. If the Foreign and Commonwealth Office has become involved, through the applicants notifying their local authority in advance, the papers will be sent to them, who will pass them on to the Home Office. Otherwise they will be sent directly to the Home Office Immigration Department, who will in due course send them to the Department of Health.

2. *Entry Clearance Considerations*

After seeking advice from the Department of Health through the local authority, the entry clearance requirements, as assessed by the entry clearance officer, are that:

(i) there has been a genuine transfer of parental responsibility from the natural parents;

(ii) the adoption was not fraudulent; and

(iii) the foreign adoption has not taken place to facilitate entrance into the United Kingdom.

The entry clearance officer will also have to be satisfied that:

(i) the child can be maintained and accommodated by the applicants without reliance upon public funds;

(ii) the child will be living with the applicants;

(iii) the applicants are themselves settled in the United Kingdom and one of them is a British citizen;

(iv) the proposed adoption is in the child's best interest.

Thus, in *Re W* [1985] 3 W.L.R. 945 (see App. 5), an aunt's application to adopt her nephew was to safeguard her long-term future as a British citizen and so that he could keep her in old age and not to promote his welfare during the remainder of his childhood. The adoption application was therefore refused.

The entry clearance officer will also not allow a child to enter the country without being sure that the adoption is likely to be a success. For that reason, he might want to consider the local authority assessment report to consider the child's chances of success before granting entry clearance. Where that report has not yet been produced, entry clearance can still be granted for a limited period of time, but he will still want to consider the plans for the child and, if possible, evaluate their success.

The entire process can take many months, depending upon what advance notice has been provided by the applicants and whether the documents are in sufficient order.

The applicants will be looked upon as sponsors of the child for immigration purposes. Only when a domestic adoption order is made will they be seen as the child's parents.

3. *Formalities*

When granted, entry clearance can take the form of either a visa or an entry certificate, which will be placed in the child's passport.

If the child does not at that stage have a passport, one must be obtained in his country of origin. The passport is most likely to be granted by that country's equivalent of the Home Office if an adoption order has been granted in his own country and the entry clearance officer in the United Kingdom has agreed to the child's entry.

Grounds for Refusal of Entry Clearance

(1) Parental responsibility has not been genuinely transferred.

(2) A fraudulent adoption order was obtained to facilitate entry into the United Kingdom.

(3) The sponsors have adopted a child of relatives who are not dead or are living in exceptionally hard circumstances.

(4) The consent of the natural parents to the adoption is questionable.

(5) The sponsors have adopted a child who has a large number of siblings who have remained with their parents.

(6) The sponsors have adopted a child who is likely to or is actually retaining contact with his natural parents.

Examples

In *Re K (A Minor) (Adoption Order: Nationality)* [1994] 3 W.L.R. 572, the Court of Appeal stated that where an adoption application had no practical consequences for the child's welfare, it could not be a substitute for an immigration application (see App. 5).

Equally, in *Mathieu v. Entry Clearance Officer, Bridgetown* [1979-1980] Imm.A.R. 157, the adoption was one of convenience arranged simply to facilitate entry clearance of the children concerned into the United Kingdom (see App. 5).

However, in *Re H* [1982] 3 W.L.R. 501, it was said that where the court believed there had been a genuine transfer of parental responsibility and a wish to keep the child as a member of the family, immigration requirements had been complied with (see App. 5).

The Appeal Process

See Chapter 12, dealing with appeals generally.

Chapter 9

IMMIGRATION CHECKLIST

The following is intended as a quick guide to some of the issues and terms that are relevant to the immigration procedure for an adopted child.

Citizenship

(1) Where a court of England and Wales makes an adoption order in favour of a parent who is a British citizen, the child will automatically become a British citizen.

(2) An adoption order made outside the United Kingdom has no automatic effect on citizenship, but will grant citizenship once the order is recognised in a United Kingdom court, if the parent whom the registration order favours is a British citizen.

(3) Commonwealth citizens who have been legally adopted by a parent who was born in the United Kingdom, by virtue of either a court order in the United Kingdom or an overseas adoption, will be deemed for right of abode purposes to be a British citizen.

(4) A new-born infant abandoned in the United Kingdom will be deemed to have been born in the United Kingdom to a parent who at the time of his birth was a British citizen or settled in the United Kingdom.

(5) A child born in the United Kingdom who did not become a British citizen at birth is entitled to be registered as a British citizen if, while he is a minor, his father or mother becomes a British citizen or settles in the United Kingdom and an application is made for the child's registration.

(6) An annulment or revocation of an adoption order will not revoke a child's British citizenship.

(7) An adoption order made by a court in the Channel Islands or the Isle of Man will not confer British citizenship.

Domicile

(1) The domicile of a person for the purpose of adoption law is determined by the law of England and Wales.

(2) "Domicile of origin" is the domicile acquired by a child at birth by operation of law and will be the domicile of the person upon whom the child is legally dependent.

(3) A child born in wedlock, or to a father who is not married to his mother but who has parental responsibility at the date of his birth, will take the domicile of his father; a child born out of wedlock, whose father does not have parental responsibility for him, will take the domicile of his mother.

(4) A "domicile of choice" is acquired when a person resides in a country with the intention of continuing to reside there for an indefinite period of time, coupled with the absence of an intention to return to reside permanently in his previous domicile.

(5) A "domicile of dependency" is determined by reference to the domicile of one or other of the child's parents.

Parental Responsibility

(1) An adopted child will be treated as a natural child for settlement purposes where there has been a genuine transfer of parental responsibility from the natural parents to the adoptive parents.

(2) For immigration purposes the onus rests on the adoptive parents to prove the transfer of parental responsibility was genuine.

(3) Even where a legal adoption is lacking, a child will be granted leave to enter the United Kingdom if he has been treated as a member of the family by the applicants.

(4) The Home Secretary can exercise his discretion to allow any child to enter the United Kingdom from abroad.

Chapter 10

WHEN IMMIGRATION PROCEDURES ARE NOT FOLLOWED

Whilst a system has come into being to regularise adoption applications relating to children from abroad, suggested procedures are not always followed. Children still arrive at ports of entry without visas and without adoption orders.

Airlines can now be fined for allowing anyone to travel without the required permits for the port of entry. This prohibition also relates to children's carers or intended adoptive parents.

It is anticipated that a criminal offence will be enacted in the new Adoption Act of bringing a child to the United Kingdom for adoptive purposes without first obtaining proper legal clarification.

Temporary Entry Clearance

1. *Child Arriving Alone*

When a child arrives without the proper documentation, it is unlikely that the immigration officer will turn the child back if he has a sponsor in the form of prospective adoptive parents with British citizenship or who are already settled in the United Kingdom.

The immigration officer will want to clarify that the applicants wish to adopt the child in question. It is unlikely that the immigration officer will grant clearance in whatever form without some genuine inquiry as to the applicants' commitment to the child.

Limited leave to enter and remain is likely to be granted so that the local authority can be advised of the intended adoption application and prepare their assessment report.

2. *Child Arriving with Adult*

Where a child arrives at a port of entry with an adult who is also seeking entry clearance and neither have the necessary documentary evidence, the presence of the child could assist the adult in obtaining limited leave to enter and remain, as officers are confident of turning back adults but not children.

If the adult states he wishes to adopt that child, the immigration officer prior to granting any limited immigration relief will want to clarify the exact intention and commitment of the adult towards the child. It is not unknown for adults to make false representations as to their intention to adopt the child accompanying them in order to facilitate entry into the United Kingdom.

If a child has been granted leave to remain for the purpose of adoption and is in due course abandoned by the applicants, the local authority will be responsible for the child. For the local authority's duties in such a case, see Chapter 7.

The Purpose of the Adoption Application

A child will not be granted entry into the United Kingdom if the sole purpose of a proposed adoption is to circumvent the immigration rules.

Children brought into England and Wales from war zones such as the former Yugoslavia to stay with relatives, for example, are unlikely to be able to be adopted by those relatives if the court believes that the purpose of the application is to facilitate entry for the duration of the war. Courts will be suspicious of such applications even if the child's parents have given their consent to the adoption. The situation would, of course, be different if the natural parents could be shown to have abandoned the child.

In a case where an adult relative or friend applies to adopt a child who has leave to stay temporarily in the United Kingdom for the purpose of study, for example, the court will also have to consider whether the application is to circumvent the immigration rules.

Chapter 11

REMOVING A CHILD FROM THE JURISDICTION FOR ADOPTION ABROAD

A person who is not domiciled in the United Kingdom may remove a child from the United Kingdom if an application to do so has been made and the court is satisfied that the child is to be adopted by the applicant under the law of or within the country where the applicant is domiciled (Adoption Act, s.55). The English court will make an order giving the applicant parental responsibility for the child. If no such order has been obtained, it is an offence to remove the child for adoption abroad (Adoption Act, s.56).

If the child is in the care of a local authority, they may arrange for the child to emigrate, with the approval of the court, by virtue of the Children Act 1989, Sched. 2, para. 19.

Procedure

An originating application must be issued in the county court, with an accompanying affidavit giving details of the length of time that the applicants have known the child and in what capacity, where the child will live and how he will be kept financially.

Expert evidence relating to the adoption law of the country where the applicant is domiciled must be filed, in translation if it is not an English-speaking country. Evidence of the applicant's domicile and the length thereof must be shown.

A Guardian *ad litem* will be appointed to act as the child's representative.

This procedure is mandatory. In *Re M (An Infant Adoption: Removal from Jurisdiction)* [1973] 1 All E.R. 852, the applicants were married and domiciled in Denmark and wanted to adopt an illegitimate child who was living with foster parents. Under wardship proceedings, they sought to remove the child to Denmark and have continuous care of her, before returning to England to apply for a provisional adoption order. Their application for removal was refused as a child cannot be removed for adoption or as part of a step in the process of adoption, unless the applicants are the child's guardians or have the Secretary of State's consent to the removal. (See further, App. 5.)

The Role of the Local Authority

The local authority has the same involvement as for a domestic application, providing a Schedule 2 report on the applicants' suitability.

The local authority may also be in contact with their counterpart abroad regarding the prospective placement, in which case all information and correspondence must be made available to the court.

The local authority can arrange for a child in its care to reside temporarily outside of England, with the court's consent (Children Act 1989, Sched. 2, para. 19). It can also arrange for a child to live abroad who is not in care, but who is looked after by the local authority, if all persons with parental responsibility agree (*ibid.*).

Considerations of the Court

The matter will proceed as for a domestic adoption application, in that the court must be satisfied that all the requirements of the Adoption Act 1976 have been met.
These are that:

(i) the child is to be adopted within the law or in the country where the applicant is domiciled (s.55);

(ii) the parent or guardian of the child consents to the removal or such consent has been dispensed with (s.16(1));

(iii) where the child understands the situation, he consents;

(iv) the local authority has seen the child with the applicant;

(v) the arrangements for the adoption have been made by a permitted person or body (s.11);

(vi) no prohibited payments have been made (s.57);

(vii) the welfare of the child has been considered and living abroad with the applicant is in his best interest;

(viii) proper arrangements have been made in the country where the applicant is domiciled.

In *Re C (Minors: Adoption by Relative)* [1989] 1 W.L.R. 61, two children were made wards of court and received into the local authority's care. They were placed with long-term foster parents with a view to adoption. The paternal great uncle and great aunt, domiciled in Australia, then sought to remove them there. They were considered to be suitable adopters by the local authority, even though a great uncle does come within the definition of a relative in section 72 of the Adoption Act 1976 (see further, App. 5).

Registration and Citizenship

A copy of the order made under section 55 must be sent to the Adopted Children Register, even though the child is going to live abroad (Adoption Act, s.50).

If the child is a British citizen, he will remain so, even if the applicants do not have British citizenship (Nationality Act 1981, s.1(1)).

Chapter 12

APPEALS

A. Immigration Appeals

Challenging an immigration decision can be done by appeal, judicial review or by an attempt to ward the child concerned. The following procedures should be considered.

1. *Decisions liable to appeal*

Any of the following decisions could be subject to the appeals procedure. The first of these will be most commonly encountered by applicants seeking entry to the United Kingdom. In any case, reference should be made to works specifically dealing with Immigration law.

(i) Refusal of entry clearance.

(ii) Refusal of leave to enter.

(iii) Refusal to vary leave to remain.

(iv) Refusal to extend leave to remain.

(v) A deportation order.

(vi) Refusal to revoke a deportation order.

(vii) The validity of directions to remove an illegal immigrant.

(viii) Removal to a particular country or destination.

2. *Refusal of entry clearance*

Where a British citizen seeks to being a child into the country without prior immigration entry clearance, the child can technically be refused entry. If the adoptive parents are not British and also do not have entry clearance, they can both be refused entry.

If a child arrives at the point of entry without prior entry clearance and the immigration officer refuses entry, the child is likely to be returned to his country of origin where the appeal against the immigration officer's decision can be made. A child could technically be granted temporary admission in these circumstances. This is not the same as limited leave to remain, as the former (which will only be for a very short time) requires that any appeal be made to the adjudicator from outside the jurisdiction, while the latter allows for an appeal from within the jurisdiction.

Article 8 of the European Convention on Human Rights guarantees the right to respect for family life. However unmeritorious an applicant's immigration history, in countries which have incorporated the Convention into their domestic law, the European Court of Human Rights would probably consider an immigration decision separating an applicant from his child as in breach of that Article. As the United Kingdom has not incorporated the Convention, it cannot be relied upon in these circumstances. However, the Home Office has directed immigration officers to have regard to Article 8 because of the positive attitude that the European Court has towards it.

Procedure

An application for entry clearance should first have been made to the entry clearance officer at the Consulate or Embassy abroad. If that application is refused, the appeal application should be lodged at the same establishment.

The same procedure should be followed where, (i) there has been refusal of entry into the United Kingdom when the child has arrived without entry clearance; (ii) there has been refusal of entry when the child has arrived with entry clearance; and (iii) there has been part refusal of leave to enter, for example by allowing temporary entry only.

The appeal documentation will be sent to the United Kingdom for consideration by an adjudicator of the Immigration Appeal Tribunal.

Where the child is in England, the appeal should be through the Appeals Section of the Home Office, at Lunar House, Croydon, CR9 2BY, which will process the appeal and have it listed before an Immigration Appeal Tribunal.

Once the appeal has been lodged, an acknowledgement letter will be sent to the appellant. Where the appellant is in England, that letter will allow him to remain until the outcome of the appeal.

Where the Home Secretary himself decides that the child should not be allowed entry or to remain in England, there is no right of appeal.

3. Wardship

In the past, applicants have sought to ward children when an entry clearance officer, immigration officer or even an adjudicator has refused leave to enter or remain in England. This has been criticised as an attempt to fetter their discretion and is not a sensible route for obtaining entrance.

An attempt to ward a child can only be made if the child is in England. If the wardship court does agree to ward the child, it is only likely to do so pending the outcome of the immigration or adoption decision. It will not override either process.

Procedure

Issue an originating summons in the High Court with an accompanying affidavit, stating:

(a) the child's country of origin;

(b) whether the child has already been adopted in another country;

(c) why immigration clearance has been refused;

(d) whether clarification of the immigration position is still awaited;

(e) the position of the adoptive parents.

Case law

In *Re A (An Infant)* and *Re S (N) (An Infant)* [1968] 2 All E.R. 145, the Court said that it would not exercise its wardship jurisdiction to interfere with statutory immigration controls. (See further, App. 5.)

In *Re A* [1992] 1 F.L.R. 427, the Court found that the only reason for the wardship application was to try and fetter the power of the Home Secretary regarding the immigration status of the father applying to adopt the child in question. (See further, App. 5.)

In *Re F (A Minor)* [1989] 3 W.L.R. 691, it was held that the wardship application was an abuse of process, designed to keep a child who had overstayed his period for leave to enter in the country. (See further, App. 5.)

4. *Judicial Review*

It is possible to judicially review both the decision of the entry clearance officer and of the adjudicator of the Immigration Appeal Tribunal. Judicial review is a procedure in the High Court that challenges the validity of the decision making process. It must be shown that the officer or adjudicator has exercised his function outside of the Immigration Rules, that is not in accordance with his powers.

The usual grounds are as follows.

(i) The entry clearance officer or adjudicator was wrong in law.

(ii) There have been procedural defects in respect of the application.

(iii) The decision was made irrationally or illegally.

As with wardship proceedings, the Court is unlikely to judicially review a tribunal's decision unless an administrative error can be shown. Otherwise, it will probably consider that the application is only being made to facilitate entry clearance. Thus, in *R. v. Secretary of State, ex p. Luff* [1992] 1 F.L.R. 59, an application for judicial review of the Home Secretary's refusal to allow entry was refused as the advice the Home Secretary relied upon from the Department of Health in making the immigration decision was rational advice (see further, App. 5).

Procedure

The ordinary judicial review procedure must be followed.

B. Refusal to Allow Adoption

Where the court refuses to make an adoption order within its jurisdiction, an appeal to the Court of Appeal can be lodged if it can be argued that the judge at first instance erred upon a point of law.

The usual procedure for appeal to the Court of Appeal must be followed.

Chapter 13

ANNULMENT AND REVOCATION OF ADOPTION ORDERS

An application for the annulment or revocation of an adoption order is governed by section 53(1) of the Adoption Act 1976 (see App. 2A).

Preliminary Procedure

In an application for revocation, an originating summons in Form 9 (see App. 3G) should be issued out of the Principal Registry or otherwise out of a High Court Registry.

If the application is for an order is to be declared invalid, then it is by way of originating summons in Form 10.

The party filing the application for the annulment or the revocation will be the applicant. The adopted child and any other interested person other than the applicant will be a respondent.

The application has to be issued within two years of the date of the adoption order. If the application is made outside the two-year time limit, leave must first be obtained from the court.

An affidavit supporting the case must be issued within 14 days of the application. Where expert evidence as to the internal law of a foreign country was considered when the original adoption order was made, the affidavit must exhibit that evidence.

1. *The Official Solicitor*

The Official Solicitor will act as the child's guardian where the child is under the age of 18 at the time of the application to revoke or annul the adoption order. The welfare of the child will be his prime consideration.

2. *The Local Authority*

The court will look at the original homestudy report and the Schedule 2 report. It is also likely to want an update report containing the local authority's view as to whether there should be an annulment or revocation.

Legal Considerations

The court will consider the internal law of the foreign country of which the applicant was a national, where the interpretation of its statutes relating to adoption might have prevented the order being made.

The court will also consider any question of whether the consent of the natural parents was properly given before the adoption order was made in that foreign country.

The adoption order in England and Wales may be deemed to be contrary to public policy. For example, the action of certain parents in abducting children from abroad then seeking to adopt them would have to be condemned and could result in past orders being revoked or annulled.

The Hearing

Notice of the hearing must be given in the same way and to the same parties as required under the procedure for a Convention adoption or an ordinary adoption.

At the hearing, the court will hear argument and then make its decision.

If annulment or revocation is deemed not to be in the interest of the child, even if there has been an element of deception, the court may retain the status quo and refuse to annul or revoke.

Service of Order

When the order has been made, it must be served upon the same parties as is required under the procedure for Convention adoptions or ordinary adoptions.

Citizenship

Loss of citizenship does not automatically result from revocation or annulment of an adoption order (Adoption Act 1976, s.40(3)). The Home Office may wish to make its own inquiries as to the legal status of the person who was or remains a child at the time the revocation order is make.

Chapter 14

THE WAY FORWARD: A NEW LAW

The Government's intentions regarding Intercountry Adoption are set out in the White paper, *Adoption: The Future*, November 1993. If the White Paper becomes an Act of Parliament in due course, the procedure for adopting a child from abroad will have been put on a proper footing, something that can only be commended.

Those countries who have not already done so will be encouraged to become signatories of the Hague Convention on Protection of Children and Co-operation in Respect of Intercountry Adoption 1993 (the 1993 Convention), just as they have become signatories of the Hague Convention on International Child Abduction 1984. The 1993 Convention will become law through a new Adoption Act, just as the 1984 Convention became law through the Child Abduction and Custody Act 1985.

It is hoped that there will be mutual recognition of adoption orders between signatory countries. Standards and procedures in all intercountry adoptions with other Convention countries should conform with the principles of the Convention. There ought to be mutual arrangements for dealing with children who may be adopted and for assessing the parent applicants. The sending country will be responsible for the child, and the receiving country will remain responsible for the parent applicants.

Most importantly, there will be no need for recourse to the English courts when an adoption order has already been made in a country that is a signatory of the 1993 Convention. An adoption order under the 1993 Convention will not require repetition of any court process whatsoever.

Immigration considerations will be made part of the adoption procedure. A child will not be able to be adopted abroad without the immigration requirements being met, first in the sending country and then in the receiving country. The foreign court will demand proof that immigration officers will allow the child into England and Wales before making its own adoption order and allowing the child to emigrate.

Particularly important Articles of the 1993 Convention, which is set out in Appendix 1C, are:

(a) Article 4: the consent of the natural parents.

(b) Article 5: the authorisation of the child's entering and remaining permanently in the receiving country.

(c) Article 6: the central authority which, in so far as England and Wales is concerned, will not be the same central authority as for international child abduction.

(d) Article 9: the task of the central authority.

(e) Article 14: prospective adopters who are habitually resident in their country can seek to adopt a child from abroad by first applying to their central authority.

(f) Article 15: the central authority will prepare a report upon the prospective parents' suitability and send the report to the central authority of the State of origin.

(g) Article 16: the central authority of the State of origin will prepare its own report that will deal with all domestic criteria before adoption.

(h) Article 17: there will only be consent by the state of origin where there has been consent from the natural parents; the adoption will only proceed where there has been the agreement of both central authorities and there will then be authorisation for the child to enter the receiving country.

(i) Article 18: the central authorities will be the bodies dealing with emigration of the child from the state of origin and subsequent entry into the receiving state.

(j) Article 21: the central authority will seek to withdraw a child where placement is not in his best interest.

(k) Article 22: the central authority may delegate its function to a body of professional competence.

(l) Article 23: an adoption certified by the competent authority of the state of adoption as having been made in accordance with the Convention shall be recognised by operation of law in the other contracting states.

(m) Article 24: the recognition of the adoption may be refused in a Contracting state if the adoption is manifestly contrary to public policy.

(n) Article 33: if any provision of the Convention has not been respected, the central authority should be informed.

The central authority in England will clearly be responsible for co-ordinating applications and their process and liaising with the central authority of the foreign, sending country. It will operate in the same manner as the central authority that presently exists for child abduction proceedings at the Official Solicitor's Department under the umbrella of the Lord Chancellor's Department, and is expected to be organised through the Department of Health.

List of Appendices

Appendix I

INTERNATIONAL MATERIALS

A. HAGUE CONVENTION CONCERNING THE POWERS OF AUTHORITIES AND THE LAW APPLICABLE IN RESPECT OF THE PROTECTION OF INFANTS 1961

The States signatory to the present Convention,

Desiring to establish common provision on the powers of authorities and the law applicable in respect of the protection of infants,

Have resolved to conclude a Convention to this effect and have agreed upon the following provisions:

Article 1

The judicial or administrative authorities of the State of the habitual residence of an infant have power, subject to the provisions of articles 3 and 4, and paragraph 3 of article 5 of the present Convention, to take measures directed to the protection of his person or property.

Article 2

The authorities having power by virtue of the terms of article 1 shall take the measures provided by the domestic law.

That law shall determine the conditions for the initiation, modification and termination of the said measures. It shall also govern their effects both in respect of relations between the infant and the persons or institutions responsible for his care, and in respect of third persons.

Article 3

A relationship subjecting the infant to authority, which arises directly from the domestic law of the State of the infant's nationality, shall be recognised in all the contracting States.

Article 4

If the authorities of the State of the infant's nationality consider that the interests of the infant so require, they may, after having informed the authorities of the State of his habitual residence, take measures according to their own law for the protection of his person or property.

That law shall determine the conditions for the initiation, modification and termination of the said measures. It shall also govern their effects both in respect of relations between the infant and the persons or institutions responsible for his care, and in respect of third persons.

The measures taken by virtue of the preceding paragraphs of the present article shall replace any measures which may have been taken by the authorities of the State where the infant has his habitual residence.

Article 5

If the habitual residence of an infant is transferred from one contracting State to another, measures taken by the authorities of the State of the former habitual residence shall remain in force in so far as the authorities of the new habitual residence have not terminated or replaced them.

Measures taken by the authorities of the State of the former habitual residence shall be terminated or replaced only after previous notice to the said authorities.

In the case of change of residence of an infant who was under the protection of authorities of the State of his nationality, measures taken by them according to their domestic law shall remain in force in the State of the new habitual residence.

Article 6

The authorities of the State of the infant's nationality may, in agreement with those of the State where he has his habitual residence or where he possesses property, entrust to them the putting into force of the measures taken.

The authorities of the State of the habitual residence of the infant may do the same with regard to the authorities of the State where the infant possesses property.

Article 7

The measures taken by the competent authorities by virtue of the preceding articles of the present Convention shall be recognised in all contracting States. However, if these measures involve acts of enforcement in a State other than that in which they have been taken, their recognition and enforcement shall be governed either by the domestic law of the country in which enforcement is sought, or by the relevant international conventions.

Article 8

Notwithstanding the provisions of articles 3 and 4, and paragraph 3 of article 5 of the present Convention, the authorities of the State of the infant's habitual residence may take measures of protection in so far as the infant is threatened by serious danger to his person or property.

The authorities of the other contracting States are not bound to recognise these measures.

Article 9

In all cases of urgency, the authorities of any contracting State in whose territory the infant or his property is, may take any necessary measures of protection.

When the authorities which are competent according to the present Convention shall have taken the steps demanded by the situation, measures taken theretofore.

Article 10

In order to ensure the continuity of the measures applied to the infant, the authorities of a contracting State shall, as far as possible, not take measures with respect to him save after an exchange of views with the authorities of the other contracting States whose decisions are still in force.

Article 11

All authorities who have taken measures by virtue of the provisions of the present Convention shall without delay inform the authorities of the State of the infant's nationality of them and, where appropriate, those of the State of his habitual residence.

Each contracting State shall designate the authorities which can directly give and receive the information envisaged in the previous paragraph. It shall give notice of such designation to the Ministry of Foreign Affairs of the Netherlands.

Article 12

For the purposes of the present Convention "infant" shall mean any person who has that status, in accordance with both the domestic law of the State of his nationality and that of his habitual residence.

Article 13

The present Convention shall apply to all infants who have their habitual residence in one of the contracting States.

Nevertheless any powers conferred by the present Convention on the authorities of the State of the infant's nationality shall be reserved to the contracting States.

Each contracting State may reserve the right to limit the application of the present Convention to infants who are nationals of one of the contracting States.

Article 14

For the purposes of the present Convention, if the domestic law of the infant's nationality consists of a non-unified system, "the domestic law of the State of the infant's nationality" and "authorities of the State of the infant's nationality," shall mean respectively the law and the authorities determined by the rules and force in that system and, failing any such rules, that law and those authorities within such system with which the infant has the closest connexion.

Article 15

Each contracting State may reserve the jurisdiction of its authorities empowered to decide on a petition for annulment, dissolution or modification of the marital relationship of the parents of an infant, to take measures for the protection of his person or property.

Article 16

The application of the provisions of the present Convention can only be refused in the contracting States if such application is manifestly contrary to public policy.

Article 17

The present Convention applies only to measures taken after its entry into force.

The relationships subjecting the infant to authority which arise directly from the domestic law of the State of the infant's nationality shall be recognised from the date of entry into force of the Convention.

Article 18

In relations between the contracting States the present Convention replaces the Convention governing the *tutelle* of infants, signed at The Hague on 12 June, 1902.

It shall not affect any provisions of other conventions binding the contracting States at the time of its entry into force.

Article 19

The present Convention is open to the signature of the States represented at the Ninth Session of the Hague Conference on Private International Law.

It shall be ratified and the instruments of ratification deposited with the Ministry of Foreign Affairs of The Netherlands.

Article 20

The present Convention shall enter into effect the sixtieth day after the deposit of the third instrument of ratification contemplated in article 19, paragraph 2.

As respects each signatory State subsequently ratifying the Convention, it shall enter into effect on the sixtieth day from the date of the deposit of its instrument of ratification.

Article 21

Any State not represented at the Ninth Session of the Hague Conference on Private International Law may adhere to the present Convention after it has entered into effect in virtue of article 20, paragraph 1. The instrument of adhesion shall be deposited with the Ministry of Foreign Affairs of The Netherlands.

The adhesion shall have effect only in the relations between the adhering State and contracting States which declare that they accept this adhesion. The acceptance shall be notified to the Ministry of Foreign Affairs of The Netherlands.

Between the adhering State and the State which has declared that it accepts the adhesion the Convention shall enter into effect the sixtieth day after the notification mentioned in the preceding paragraph.

Article 22

At the moment of the signature, ratification or adhesion, each State may declare that the present Convention shall extend to all the territories which it represents on the international level, or to one or more of them. This declaration shall have effect at the moment of the entry into effect of the Convention for that State.

Thereafter, any extension of this nature shall be notified to the Ministry of Foreign Affairs of The Netherlands.

When the declaration of extension is made on the occasion of a signature or ratification, the Convention shall enter into effect for the territories indicated in conformity with the provisions of article 20. When the declaration of extension is made on the occasion of an adhesion, the Convention shall enter into effect for the territories indicated in conformity with the provisions article 21.

Article 23

At the latest at the moment of ratification or adhesion, each State may make the reserves contemplated in articles 13, paragraph 3, and 15, paragraph 1 of this Convention. No other reserve shall be admitted.

When notifying an extension of the Convention in conformity with article 22, each State also may make these reserves with an effect limited to the territories, or some of them, indicated in the extension.

At any time, each contracting State may withdraw a reserve made. Such withdrawal shall be notified to the Ministry of Foreign Affairs of The Netherlands.

The effect of the reserve shall cease the sixtieth day after the notification mentioned in the preceding paragraph.

Article 24

The present Convention shall have a duration of five years starting from the date of its entry into effect in conformity with article 20, paragraph 1, even for States which have ratified it or adhered hereto subsequently.

The Convention shall be renewed tacitly every five years, in the absence of a denunciation.

The denunciation must be notified at least six months before the expiration of the five years period to the Ministry of Foreign Affairs of The Netherlands.

It may be limited to certain of the territories to which the Convention applies.

The denunciation shall have effect only as regards the State which shall have given notice of it. The Convention shall remain in force for the other contracting States.

Article 25

The Ministry of Foreign Affairs of The Netherlands shall give notice to the States indicated in article 19, as well as to States which will have adhered in conformity with the provisions of article 21, of:

(a) notifications dealt with in article 11, paragraph 2;

(b) signatures and ratifications dealt with in article 19;

(c) the date at which this Convention will enter into effect in conformity with the provisions of article 20, paragraph 1;

(d) adhesions and acceptances dealt with in article 21 and the date at which they will take effect;

(e) extensions dealt with in article 22 and the date at which they will take effect;

(f) reserves and withdrawals of reserves dealt with in article 23;

(g) denunciations dealt with in article 24, paragraph 3.

IN WITNESS WHEREOF, the undersigned, being duly authorised, have signed the present Convention.

DONE at The Hague, on 5 October 1961, in a single copy, which shall be deposited in the archives of the Government of The Netherlands. A certified true copy shall be sent, through the diplomatic channel, to each of the States represented at the Ninth Session of the Hague Conference on Private International Law.

B. HAGUE CONVENTION ON JURISDICTION, APPLICABLE LAW AND RECOGNITION OF DECREES RELATING TO ADOPTIONS 1965

The States signatory to the present Convention,

Desiring to establish common provisions on jurisdiction, applicable law and recognition of decrees relating to adoption,

Have resolved to conclude a Convention to this effect and have agreed upon the following provisions:

Article 1

The present Convention applies to an adoption between:

on the one hand, a person who, possessing the nationality of one of the contracting States, has his habitual residence within one of these States, or spouses each of whom, possessing the nationality of one of the contracting States, has his or her habitual residence within one of these States, and

on the other hand, a child who has not attained the age of eighteen years at the time when the application for adoption is made and has not been married and who, possessing the nationality of one of the contracting States, has his habitual residence within one of these States.

Article 2

The present Convention shall not apply where—

(a) the adopters neither possess the same nationality nor have their habitual residence in the same contracting State;

(b) the adopter or adopters and the child, all possessing the same nationality, habitually reside in the State of which they are nationals;

(c) an adoption is not granted by an authority having jurisdiction under article 3.

Article 3

Jurisdiction to grant an adoption is vested in—

(a) the authorities of the State where the adopter habitually resides or, in the case of an adoption by spouses, the authorities of the State in which both habitually reside;

(b) the authorities of the State of which the adopter is a national or, in the case of an adoption by spouses, the authorities of the State of which both are nationals.

The conditions relating to habitual residence and nationality must be fulfilled both at the time when the application for adoption is made and at the time when the adoption is granted.

Article 4

The authorities who have jurisdiction under the first paragraph of article 3 shall, subject to the provisions of the first paragraph of article 5, apply their internal law to the conditions governing an adoption.

Nevertheless, an authority having jurisdiction by virtue of habitual residence shall respect any provision prohibiting adoption contained in the national law of the adopter or, in the case of an adoption by spouses, any such provision of their common national law, if such a prohibition has been referred to in a declaration of the kind contemplated in article 13.

Article 5

The authorities who have jurisdiction under the first paragraph of article 3 shall apply the national law of the child relating to consents and consultations, other than those with respect to an adopter, his family or his or her spouse.

If according to the said law the child or a member of his family must appear in person before the authority granting the adoption, the authority shall, if the person concerned is not habitually resident in the State of that authority, proceed, where appropriate, by means of a *commission rogatoire.*

Article 6

The authorities referred to in the first paragraph of article 3 shall not grant an adoption unless it will be in the interest of the child. Before granting an adoption they shall carry out, through the agency of the appropriate local authorities, a thorough inquiry relating to the adopter or adopters, the child and his family. As far as possible, this inquiry shall be carried out in co-operation with public or private organisations qualified in the field of inter-country adoptions and the help of social workers having special training or having particular experience concerning the problems of adoption.

The authorities of all contracting States shall promptly give all the assistance requested for the purposes of an adoption governed by the present Convention; for this purpose the authorities may communicate directly with each other.

Each contracting State may designate one or more authorities empowered to communicate in accordance with the preceding paragraph.

Article 7

Jurisdiction to annul or revoke an adoption governed by the present Convention shall be vested in—

(a) the authorities of the contracting State in which the person adopted habitually resides at the time when the application to annul or to revoke the adoption is made;

(b) the authorities of the State in which at that time the adopter habitually resides or, in the case of an adoption by spouses, both of them habitually reside;

(c) the authorities of the State which granted the adoption.

An adoption may be annulled—

(a) on any ground permitted by the internal law of the State which granted the adoption; or

(b) in accordance with the national law of the adopter or adopters at the time when that adoption was granted in cases where the application to annul is based on failure to comply with a prohibition to which the second paragraph of article 4 applies; or

(c) in accordance with the national law of the person adopted at the time when the adoption was granted in cases where the application to annul is based on failure to obtain a consent required by the law.

An adoption may be revoked in accordance with the internal law of the authority exercising jurisdiction.

Article 8

Every adoption governed by the present Convention and granted by an authority having jurisdiction under the first paragraph of article 3 shall be recognised without further formality in all contracting States.

Every decision annulling or revoking an adoption granted by an authority having jurisdiction under article 7 shall be recognised without further formality in all contracting States.

If any question arises in a contracting State with respect of the recognition of such an adoption or decision, the authorities of that State, in considering the jurisdiction of the authority which granted the adoption or which gave the decision, shall be bound by the findings of fact on which that authority based its jurisdiction.

Article 9

When an authority having jurisdiction under the first paragraph of article 3 has granted an adoption, it shall notify this fact to the other

State, if any, the authorities of which would have been empowered to grant an adoption under that article, to the State of which the child is a national to the contracting State where the child was born.

When an authority having jurisdiction under the first paragraph of article 7 has annulled or revoked an adoption, it shall notify this fact to the State the authority of which had granted the adoption, to the State of which the child is a national and to the contracting State where the child was born.

Article 10

For the purposes of the present Convention, an adopter or a child who is stateless or whose nationality is unknown, is deemed to have the nationality of the State of his habitual residence.

Article 11

For the purposes of the present Convention if in the State of which either an adopter or a child is a national, there is more than one legal system in force, references in the internal law or to the authorities of the State of which a person is a national shall be construed as references to the law or to the authorities determined by the rules in force in that State or, if there are no such rules, to the law or to authorities of that system with which the person concerned is most closely connected.

Article 12

The present Convention does not affect provisions of other Conventions relating to adoption binding contracting States at the moment of its entry into force.

Article 13

Any State may, at the time of signature, ratification or accession, with a view to the application of the second paragraph of article 4, make a declaration specifying the provisions of its internal law prohibiting adoptions founded upon—

(a) the existence of descendants of the adopter or adopters;

(b) the fact that a single person is applying to adopt;

(c) the existence of a blood relationship between an adopter and the child;

(d) the existence of a previous adoption of the child by other persons;

    (e) the requirement of a difference in age between adopter or adopters and the child;

    (f) the age of the adopter or adopters and that of the child;

    (g) the fact that the child does not reside with the adopter or adopters.

Such declarations may be revoked at any time. The revocation shall be notified to the Ministry of Foreign Affairs of the Netherlands.

Any declaration which has been revoked shall cease to have effect on the sixtieth day after the notification referred to in the preceeding paragraph.

Article 14

Any contracting State may make a declaration specifying the persons deemed to possess its nationality for the purposes of the present Convention.

Such declarations and any modification or revocation thereof shall be notified to the Ministry of Foreign Affairs of the Netherlands.

Any such declaration, modification or revocation shall have effect on the sixtieth day after the notification referred to in the preceding paragraph.

Article 15

The provisions of the present Convention may be disregarded in contracting States only when their observance would be manifestly contrary to public policy.

Article 16

Each contracting State shall designate the authorities having power—

    (a) to grant an adoption within the meaning of the first paragraph of article 3;

    (b) to exchange the communications envisaged by the second paragraph of article 6 if it is intended to make use of the power conferred by the third paragraph of article 6;

    (c) to annul or revoke an adoption under article 7;

    (d) to receive information in pursuance of article 9.

Each contracting State shall supply the Ministry of Foreign Affairs of the Netherlands with a list of the foregoing authorities and of any subsequent amendments to that list.

Article 17

With a view to the application of article 5, each contracting State shall inform the Ministry of Foreign Affairs of the Netherlands of the provisions of its internal law relating to consents and consultations.

Any State making a declaration under article 13 shall inform the said Ministry of the provisions of its internal law relating to the prohibitions specified in that declaration.

A contracting State shall inform the said Ministry of any modification of the provisions mentioned in the first and second paragraphs above.

Article 18

The present Convention shall be open for signature by the States represented at the Tenth Session of the Hague Conference on Private International Law.

It shall be ratified, and the instruments of ratification shall be deposited with the Ministry of Foreign Affairs of the Netherlands.

Article 19

The present Convention shall enter into force on the sixtieth day after the deposit of the third instrument of ratification referred to in the second paragraph of article 18.

The Convention shall enter into force for each signatory State which ratifies subsequently on the sixtieth day after the deposit of its instrument of ratification.

Article 20

Any State not represented at the Tenth Session of the Hague Conference on Private International Law may acceded to the present Convention after it has entered into force in accordance with the first paragraph of article 19. The instrument of accession shall be deposited with the Ministry of Foreign Affairs of the Netherlands.

The Convention shall enter into force for such a State in the absence of any objection from a State, which has ratified the Convention before such deposit, notified to the Ministry of Foreign Affairs of the Netherlands within a period of six months after the date on which the said Ministry has notified it of such accession.

In the absence of any such objection, the Convention shall enter into force for the acceding State on the first day of the month following the expiration of the last of the periods referred to in the preceding paragraph.

Article 21

Any State may, at the time of signature, ratification or accession, declare that the present Convention shall extend to all the territories for the international relations of which it is responsible, or to one or more of them. Such a declaration shall take effect on the date of entry into force of the Convention for the State concerned.

At any time thereafter, such extensions shall be notified to the Ministry of Foreign Affairs of the Netherlands.

The Convention shall enter into force for the territories mentioned in such an extension on the sixtieth day after the notification referred to in the preceding paragraph.

Article 22

Any State may, not later than the moment of its ratification or accession, reserve the right not to recognise an adoption granted by an authority exercising jurisdiction under sub-paragraph (b) of the first paragraph of article 3, when at the time of the application to adopt the child had his habitual residence within its own territory and did not possess the nationality of the State in which the adoption was granted. No other reservation shall be permitted.

Each contracting State may also, when notifying an extension of the Convention in accordance with article 21, make the said reservation, with its effect limited to all or some of the territories mentioned in the extension.

Each contracting State may at any time withdraw a reservation it has made. Such a withdrawal shall be notified to the Ministry of Foreign Affairs of the Netherlands.

Such a reservation shall cease to have effect on the sixtieth day after the notification referred to in the preceding paragraph.

Article 23

The present Convention shall remain in force for five years from the date of its entry into force in accordance with the first paragraph of article 19, even for States which have ratified it or acceded to it subsequently.

If there has been no denunciation, it shall be renewed tacitly every five years.

Any denunciation shall be notified to the Ministry of Foreign Affairs of the Netherlands at least six months before the end of the five year period.

It may be limited to certain of the territories to which the Convention applies.

The denunciation shall have effect only as regards the State which has notified it. The Convention shall remain in force for the other contracting States.

Article 24

The Ministry of Foreign Affairs of the Netherlands shall give notice to the State referred to in article 18, and to the States which have acceded in accordance with article 20, of the following—

(a) the declarations and revocations referred to in article 13;

(b) the declarations, modifications and revocations referred to in article 14;

(c) the designation of authorities referred to in article 16;

(d) the legal provisions and modifications thereof referred to in article 17;

(e) the signatures and ratifications referred to in article 18;

(f) the date on which the present Convention enters into force in accordance with the first paragraph of article 19;

(g) the accessions referred to in article 20 and the dates on which they take effect;

(h) the extensions referred to in article 21 and the dates on which they take effect;

(i) the reservations and withdrawals referred to in article 22;

(j) the denunciations referred to in the third paragraph of article 23.

In witness whereof the undersigned, being duly authorised thereto, have signed the present Convention.

Done at The Hague, on the 15th day of November, 1965, in the English and French languages, both texts being equally authentic, in a single copy which shall be deposited in the archives of the Government of the Netherlands, and of which a certified copy shall be sent, through the diplomatic channel, to each of the States represented at the Tenth Session of the Hague Conference on Private International Law.

C. HAGUE CONVENTION ON PROTECTION OF CHILDREN AND CO-OPERATION IN RESPECT OF INTERCOUNTRY ADOPTION 1993

The States signatory to the present Convention,

Recognising that the child, for the full and harmonious development of his or her personality, should grow up in a family environment, in an atmosphere of happiness, love and understanding,

Recalling that each State should take, as a matter of priority, appropriate measures to enable the child to remain in the care of his or her family of origin,

Recognising that intercountry adoption may offer the advantage of a permanent family to a child for whom a suitable family cannot be found in his or her State of origin,

Convinced of the necessity to take measures to ensure that intercountry adoptions are made in the best interests of the child and with respect for his or her fundamental rights, and to prevent the abduction, the sale of, or traffic in children,

Desiring to establish common provisions to this effect, taking into account the principles set forth in international instruments, in particular the *United Nations Convention on the Rights of the Child,* of 20 November 1989, and the United Nations Declaration on Social and Legal Principles relating to the Protection and Welfare of Children, with Special Reference to Foster Placement and Adoption Nationally and Internationally (General Assembly Resolution 41/85, of 3 December 1986),

Have agreed upon the following provisions—

CHAPTER 1 — SCOPE OF THE CONVENTION

Article 1

The objects of the present Convention are—

(a) to establish safeguards to ensure that intercountry adoptions take place in the best interests of the child and with respect for his or her fundamental rights as recognised in international law;

(b) to establish a system of co-operation amongst Contracting States to ensure that those safeguards are respected and thereby prevent the abduction, the sale of, or traffic in children;

(c) to secure the recognition in Contracting States of adoptions made in accordance with the Convention.

Article 2

1. The Convention shall apply where a child habitually resident in one Contracting State ('the State of origin') has been, is being, or is to be moved to another Contracting State ('the receiving State') either after his or her adoption in the State of origin by spouses or a person habitually resident in the receiving State, or for the purposes of such an adoption in the receiving State or in the State of origin.

2. The Convention covers only adoptions which create a permanent parent-child relationship.

Article 3

The Convention ceases to apply if the agreements mentioned in Article 17, sub-paragraph *c*, have not been given before the child attains the age of eighteen years.

Chapter II — Requirements for Intercountry Adoptions

Article 4

An adoption within the scope of the Convention shall take place only if the competent authorities of the State of origin—

(a) have established that the child is adoptable;

(b) have determined, after possibilities for placement of the child within the State of origin have been given due consideration, that an intercountry adoption is in the child's best interests;

(c) have ensured that

(1) the persons, institutions and authorities whose consent is necessary for adoption, have been counselled as may be necessary and duly informed of the effects of their consent, in particular whether or not an adoption will result in the termination of the legal relationship between the child and his or her family of origin,

(2) such persons, institutions and authorities have given their consent freely, in the required legal form, and expressed or evidenced in writing,

(3) the consents have not been induced by payment or compensation of any kind and have not been withdrawn, and

(4) the consent of the mother, where required, has been given only after the birth of the child; and

(d) have ensured, having regard to the age and degree of maturity of the child, that

(1) he or she has been counselled and duly informed of the effects of the adoption and of his or her consent to the adoption, where such consent is required,

(2) consideration has been given to the child's wishes and opinions,

(3) the child's consent to the adoption, where such consent is required, has been given freely, in the required legal form, and expressed or evidenced in writing, and

(4) such consent has not been induced by payment or compensation of any kind.

Article 5

An adoption within the scope of the Convention shall take place only if the competent authorities of the receiving State—

(a) have determined that the prospective adoptive parents are eligible and suited to adopt;

(b) have ensured that the prospective adoptive parents have been counselled as may be necessary; and

(c) have determined that the child is or will be authorised to enter and reside permanently in that State.

CHAPTER III — CENTRAL AUTHORITIES AND ACCREDITED BODIES

Article 6

1. A Contracting State shall designate a Central Authority to discharge the duties which are imposed by the Convention upon such authorities.

2. Federal States, States with more than one system of law or States having autonomous territorial units shall be free to appoint more than one Central Authority and to specify the territorial or personal extent of their functions. Where a State has appointed more than one Central Authority, it shall designate the Central Authority to which any communication may be addressed for transmission to the appropriate Central Authority within that State.

Article 7

1. Central Authorities shall co-operate with each other and promote co-operation amongst the competent authorities in their States to protect children and to achieve the other objects to the Convention.

2. They shall take directly all appropriate measures to—

(a) provide information as to the laws of their States concerning adoption and other general information, such as statistics and standard forms;

(b) keep one another informed about the operation of the Convention and, as far as possible, eliminate any obstacles to its application.

Article 8

Central Authorities shall take, directly or through public authorities, all appropriate measures to prevent improper financial or other gain in connection with an adoption and to deter all practices contrary to the objects of the Convention.

Article 9

Central Authorities shall take, directly or through public authorities or other bodies duly accredited in their State, all appropriate measures, in particular to—

(a) collect, preserve and exchange information about the situation of the child and the prospective adoptive parents, so far as is necessary to complete the adoption;

(b) facilitate, follow and expedite proceedings with a view to obtaining the adoption;

(c) promote the development of adoption counselling and post-adoption services in their States;

(d) provide each other with general evaluation reports about experience with intercountry adoption;

(e) reply, in so far as is permitted by the law of their State, to justified requests from other Central Authorities or public authorities for information about a particular adoption situation.

Article 10

Accreditation shall only be granted to and maintained by bodies demonstrating their competence to carry out properly the tasks with which they may be entrusted.

Article 11

An accredited body shall—

(a) pursue only non-profit objectives according to such conditions and within such limits as may be established by the competent authorities of the State of accreditation;

(b) be directed and staffed by persons qualified by their ethical standards and by training or experience to work in the field of intercountry adoption; and

(c) be subject to supervision by competent authorities of that State as to its composition, operation and financial situation.

Article 12

A body accredited in one Contracting State may act in another Contracting State only if the competent authorities of both States have authorised it to do so.

Article 13

The designation of the Central Authorities and, where appropriate, the extent of their functions, as well as the names and addresses of the accredited bodies shall be communicated by each Contracting State to the Permanent Bureau of the Hague Conference on Private International Law.

CHAPTER IV — PROCEDURAL REQUIREMENTS IN INTERCOUNTRY ADOPTION

Article 14

Persons habitually resident in a Contracting State, who wish to adopt a child habitually resident in another Contracting State, shall apply to the Central Authority in the State of their habitual residence.

Article 15

1. If the Central Authority of the receiving State is satisfied that the applicants are eligible and suited to adopt, it shall prepare a report including information about their identity, eligibility and suitability to adopt, background, family and medical history, social environment, reasons for adoption, ability to undertake and intercountry adoption, as well as the characteristics of the children for whom they would be qualified to care.

2. It shall transmit the report to the Central Authority of the State of origin.

Article 16

1. If the Central Authority of the State of origin is satisfied that the child is adoptable, it shall—

(a) prepare a report including information about his or her identity, adoptability, background, social environment, family history, medical history including that of the child's family, and any special needs of the child;

(b) give due consideration to the child's upbringing and to his or her ethnic, religious and cultural background;

(c) ensure that consents have been obtained in accordance with Article 4; and

(d) determine, on the basis in particular of the reports relating to the child and the prospective adoptive parents, whether the envisaged placement is in the best interests of the child.

2. It shall transmit to the Central Authority of the receiving State its report on the child, proof that the necessary consents have been obtained and the reasons for its determination on the placement, taking care not to reveal the identity of the mother and the father if, in the State of origin, these identities may not be disclosed.

Article 17

Any decision in the State of origin that a child should be entrusted to prospective adoptive parents may only be made if—

(a) the Central Authority of that State has ensured that the prospective adoptive parents agree;

(b) the Central Authority of the receiving State has approved such decision, where such approval is required by the law of that State or by the Central Authority of the State of origin;

(c) the Central Authorities of both States have agreed that the adoption may proceed; and

(d) it has been determined, in accordance with Article 5, that the prospective adoptive parents are eligible and suited to adopt and that the child is or will be authorised to enter and reside permanently in the receiving State.

Article 18

The Central Authorities of both States shall take all necessary steps to obtain permission for the child to leave the State of origin and to enter and reside permanently in the receiving State.

Article 19

1. The transfer of the child to the receiving State may only be carried out if the requirements of Article 17 have been satisfied.

2. The Central Authorities of both States shall ensure that this transfer takes place in secure and appropriate circumstances and, if possible, in the company of the adoptive or prospective adoptive parents.

3. If the transfer of the child does not take place, the reports referred to in Articles 15 and 16 are to be sent back to the authorities who forwarded them.

Article 20

The Central Authorities shall keep each other informed about the adoption process and the measures taken to complete it, as well as about the progress of the placement if a probationary period is required.

Article 21

1. Where the adoption is to take place after the transfer of the child to the receiving State and it appears to the Central Authority of that State that the continued placement of the child with the prospective adoptive parents is not in the child's best interests, such Central Authority shall take the measures necessary to protect the child, in particular—

(a) to cause the child to be withdrawn from the prospective adoptive parents and to arrange temporary care;

(b) in consultation with the Central Authority of the State of origin, to arrange without delay a new placement of the child with a view to adoption or, if this is not appropriate, to arrange alternative long-term care; an adoption shall not take place until the Central Authority of the State of origin has been duly informed concerning the new prospective adoptive parents;

(c) as a last resort, to arrange the return of the child, if his or her interests so require.

2. Having regard in particular to the age and degree of maturity of the child, he or she shall be consulted and, where appropriate, his or consent obtained in relation to measures to be taken under this Article.

Article 22

1. The functions of a Central Authority under this Chapter may be performed by public authorities or by bodies accredited under Chapter III, to the extent permitted by the law of its State.

2. Any Contracting State may declare to the depositary of the Convention that the functions of the Central Authority under Articles 15 to 21 may be performed in that State, to the extent permitted by the law and subject to the supervision of the competent authorities of that State, also by bodies or persons who—

(a) meet the requirements of integrity, professional competence, experience and accountability of that State; and

(b) are qualified by their ethical standards and by training or experience to work in the field of intercountry adoption.

3. A Contracting State which makes the declaration provided for in paragraph 2 shall keep the Permanent Bureau of the Hague Conference on Private International Law informed of the names and addresses of these bodies and persons.

4. Any Contracting State may declare to the depositary of the Convention that adoptions of children habitually resident in its territory may only take place if the functions of the Central Authorities are performed in accordance with paragraph 1.

5. Notwithstanding any declaration made under paragraph 2, the reports provided for in Articles 15 and 16 shall, in every case, be prepared under the responsibility of the Central Authority or other authorities or bodies in accordance with paragraph 1.

CHAPTER V — RECOGNITION AND EFFECTS OF THE ADOPTION

Article 23

1. An adoption certified by the competent authority of the State of the adoption as having been made in accordance with the Convention shall be recognised by operation of law in the other Contracting States. The certificate shall specify when and by whom the agreements under Article 17, sub-paragraph *c*, were given.

2. Each Contracting State shall, at the time of signature, ratification, acceptance, approval or accession, notify the depositary of the Convention of the identity and the functions of the authority or the authorities which, in that State, are competent to make the certification. It shall also notify the depositary of any modification in the designation of these authorities.

Article 24

The recognition of an adoption may be refused in a Contracting State only if the adoption is manifestly contrary to its public policy, taking into account the best interests of the child.

Article 25

Any Contracting State may declare to the depositary of the Convention that it will not be bound under this Convention to recognise adoptions made in accordance with an agreement concluded by application of Article 39, paragraph 2.

Article 26

1. The recognition of an adoption includes recognition of

(a) the legal parent-child relationship between the child and his or her adoptive parents;

(b) parental responsibility of the adoptive parents for the child;

(c) the termination of a pre-existing legal relationship between the child and his or her mother and father, if the adoption has this effect in the Contracting State where it was made.

2. In the case of an adoption having the effect of terminating a pre-existing legal parent-child relationship, the child shall enjoy in the receiving State, and in any other Contracting State where the adoption is recognised, rights equivalent to those resulting from adoptions having this effect in each such State.

3. The preceding paragraphs shall not prejudice the application of any provision more favourable for the child, in force in the Contracting State which recognises the adoption.

Article 27

1. Where an adoption granted in the State of origin does not have the effect of terminating a pre-existing legal parent-child relationship, it may, in the receiving State which recognises the adoption under the Convention, be converted into an adoption having such an effect—

(a) if the law of the receiving State so permits; and

(b) if the consents referred to in Article 4, sub-paragraphs *c* and *d*, have been or are given for the purpose of such an adoption.

2. Article 23 applies to the decision converting the adoption.

CHAPTER VI — GENERAL PROVISIONS

Article 28

The Convention does not affect any law of a State of origin which requires that the adoption of a child habitually resident within that State take place in that State or which prohibits the child's placement in, or transfer to, the receiving State prior to adoption.

Article 29

There shall be no contact between the prospective adoptive parents and the child's parents or any other person who has care of the child until the requirements of Article 4, sub-paragraphs *a* to *c*, and Article 5, sub-paragraph *a*, have been met, unless the adoption takes place within a family or unless the contact is in compliance with the conditions established by the competent authority of the State of origin.

Article 30

1. The competent authorities of a Contracting State shall ensure that information held by them concerning the child's origin, in particular information concerning the identity of his or her parents, as well as the medical history, is preserved.

2. They shall ensure that the child or his or her representative has access to such information, under appropriate guidance, in so far as is permitted by the law of that State.

Article 31

Without prejudice to Article 30, personal data gathered or transmitted under the Convention, especially data referred to in Articles 15 and 16, shall be used only for the purposes for which they were gathered or transmitted.

Article 32

1. No one shall derive improper financial or other gain from an activity related to an intercountry adoption.

2. Only costs and expenses, including reasonable professional fees of persons involved in the adoption, may be charged or paid.

3. The directors, administrators and employees of bodies involved in an adoption shall not receive remuneration which is unreasonably high in relation to services rendered.

Article 33

A competent authority which finds that any provision of the Convention has not been respected or that there is a serious risk that it may not be respected, shall immediately inform the Central Authority of its State. This Central Authority shall be responsible for ensuring that appropriate measures are taken.

Article 34

If the competent authority of the State of destination of a document so requests, a translation certified as being in conformity with the original must be furnished. Unless otherwise provided, the costs of such translation are to be borne by the prospective adoptive parents.

Article 35

The competent authorities of the Contracting States shall act expeditiously in the process of adoption.

Article 36

In relation to a State which has two or more systems of law with regard to adoption applicable in different territorial units—

(a) any reference to habitual residence in that State shall be construed as referring to habitual residence in a territorial unit of that State;

(b) any reference to the law of that State shall be construed as referring to the law in force in the relevant territorial unit;

(c) any reference to the competent authorities or to the public authorities of that State shall be construed as referring to those authorised to act in the relevant territorial unit;

(d) any reference to the accredited bodies of that State shall be construed as referring to bodies accredited in the relevant territorial unit.

Article 37

In relation to a State which with regard to adoption has two or more systems of law applicable to different categories of persons, any reference to the law of that State shall be construed as referring to the legal system specified by the law of that State.

Article 38

A State within which different territorial units have their own rules of law in respect of adoption shall not be bound to apply the Convention where a State with a unified system of law would not be bound to do so.

Article 39

1. The Convention does not affect any international instrument to which Contracting States are Parties and which contains provisions on matters governed by the Convention, unless a contrary declaration is made by the States Parties to such instrument.

2. Any Contracting State may enter into agreements with one or more other Contracting States, with a view to improving the application of the Convention in their mutual relations. These agreements may derogate only from the provisions of Articles 14 to 16 and 18 to 21. The States which have concluded such an agreement shall transmit a copy to the depositary of the Convention.

Article 40

No reservation to the Convention shall be permitted.

Article 41

The Convention shall apply in every case where an application pursuant to Article 14 has been received after the Convention has entered into force in the receiving State and the State of origin.

Article 42

The Secretary General of the Hague Conference on Private International Law shall at regular intervals convene a Special Commission in order to review the practical operation of the Convention.

CHAPTER VII — FINAL CLAUSES

Article 43

1. The Convention shall be open for signature by the States which were Members of the Hague Conference on Private International Law at the time of its Seventeenth Session and by the other States which participated in that Session.
2. It shall be ratified, accepted or approved and the instrumer. ratification, acceptance or approval shall be deposited with the Minis-try of Foreign Affairs of the Kingdom of the Netherlands, depositary of the Convention.

Article 44

1. Any other State may accede to the Convention after it has entered into force in accordance with Article 46, paragraph 1.
2. The instrument of accession shall be deposited with the depositary.
3. Such accession shall have effect only as regards the relations between the acceding State and those Contracting States which have not raised an objection to its accession in the six months after the receipt of the notification referred to in sub-paragraph b of Article 48. Such an objection may also be raised by States at the time when they ratify, accept or approve the Convention after an accession. Any such objection shall be notified to the depositary.

Article 45

1. If a State has two or more territorial units in which different systems of law are applicable in relation to matters dealt with in the Convention, it may at the time of signature, ratification, acceptance, approval or accession declare that this Convention shall extend to all its territorial units or only to one or more of them and may modify this declaration by submitting another declaration at any time.

2. Any such declaration shall be notified to the depositary and shall state expressly the territorial units to which the Convention applies.

3. If a State makes no declaration under this Article, the Convention is to extend to all territorial units of that State.

Article 46

1. The Convention shall enter into force on the first day of the month following the expiration of three months after the deposit of the third instrument of ratification, acceptance or approval referred to in Article 43.

2. Thereafter the Convention shall enter into force—

(a) for each State ratifying, accepting or approving it subsequently, or acceding to it, on the first day of the month following the expiration of three months after the deposit of its instrument of ratification, acceptance, approval or accession;

(b) for a territorial unit to which the Convention has been extended in conformity with Article 45, on the first day of the month following the expiration of three months after the notification referred to in that Article.

Article 47

1. A State Party to the Convention may denounce it by a notification in writing addressed to the depositary.

2. The denunciation takes effect on the first day of the month following the expiration of twelve months after the notification is received by the depositary. Where a longer period for the denunciation to take effect is specified in the notification, the denunciation takes effect upon the expiration of such longer period after the notification is received by the depositary.

Article 48

The depositary shall notify the States Members of the Hague Conference on Private International Law, the other States which participated in the Seventeenth Session and the States which have acceded in accordance with Article 44, of the following—

(a) the signatures, ratifications, acceptances and approvals referred to in Article 43;

(b) the accessions and objections raised to accessions referred to in Article 44;

(c) the date on which the Convention enters into force in accordance with Article 46;

(d) the declarations and designations referred to in Articles 22, 23, 25 and 45;

(e) the agreements referred to in Article 39;

(f) the denunciations referred to in Article 47.

D. SIGNATORY COUNTRIES OF THE HAGUE CONVENTION ON INTERCOUNTRY ADOPTION 1993

Albania
Argentina
Australia
Austria
Belarus
Belgium
Benin
Bolivia
Brazil
Bulgaria
Burkina Faso
Canada
Chile
China
Colombia
Costa Rica
Czech Republic
Denmark
Ecuador
Egypt
El Salvador
Finland
France
Germany
Greece
Haiti
Honduras
Hungary
India
Indonesia
Ireland
Israel

Japan
Kenya
Lebanon
Luxembourg
Madagascar
Mauritius
Mexico
Nepal
Netherlands
Norway
Panama
Peru
Philippines
Poland
Portugal
Romania
Russia
Senegal
Slovenia
South Korea
Spain
Sri Lanka
Sweden
Switzerland
Thailand
Turkey
United Kingdom
United States of America
Uruguay
Vatican City
Venezuela
Vietnam

E. UNITED NATIONS CONVENTION ON THE RIGHTS OF THE CHILD 1989

Preamble

THE STATES PARTIES TO THE PRESENT CONVENTION,

Considering that, in accordance with the principles proclaimed in the Charter of the United Nations, recognition of the inherent dignity and of the equal and inalienable rights of all members of the human family is the foundation of freedom, justice and peace in the world,

Bearing in mind that the peoples of the United Nations have, in the Charter, reaffirmed their faith in fundamental human rights and in the dignity and worth of the human person, and have determined to promoted social progress and better standards of life in larger freedom,

Recognising that the United Nations has, in the Universal Declaration of Human Rights and in the International Covenants on Human Rights, proclaimed and agreed that everyone is entitled to all the rights and freedoms set forth therein, without distinction of any kind, such as race, colour, sex, language, religion, political or other opinion, national or social origin, property, birth or other status,

Recalling that, in the Universal Declaration of Human Rights, the United Nations has proclaimed that childhood is entitled to special care and assistance,

Convinced that the family, as the fundamental group of society and the natural environment for the growth and well-being of all its members and particularly children, should be afforded the necessary protection and assistance so that it can fully assume its responsibilities within the community,

Recognising that the child, for the full and harmonious development of his or her personality, should grow up in a family environment, in an atmosphere of happiness, love and understanding,

Considering that the child should be fully prepared to live an individual life in society, and brought up in the spirit of the ideals proclaimed in the Charter of the United Nations, and in particular in the spirit of peace, dignity, tolerance, freedom, equality and solidarity,

Bearing in mind that the need to extend particular care to the child has been stated in the Geneva Declaration of the Rights of the Child of 1924 and in the Declaration of the Rights of the Child adopted by the General Assembly on 20 November 1959 and recognised in the Universal Declaration of Human Rights, in the International Covenant on Civil and Political Rights (in particular in Articles 23 and 24), in the International Covenant on Economic, Social and Cultural Rights (in particular in Article 10) and in the statutes and relevant instruments of specialised agencies and international organisations concerned with the welfare of children,

Bearing in mind that, as indicated in the Declaration of the Rights of the Child, 'the child, by reason of his physical and mental immaturity, needs special safeguards and care, including appropriate legal protection, before as well as after birth',

Recalling the provisions of the Declaration on Social and Legal Principles relating to the Protection and Welfare of Children, with Special Reference to Foster Placement and Adoption Nationally and Internationally; the United Nations Standard Minimum Rules for the Administration of Juvenile Justice (The Beijing Rules); and the Declaration on the Protection of Women and Children in Emergency and Armed Conflict,

Recognising that, in all countries in the world, there are children living in exceptionally difficult conditions, and that such children need special consideration,

Taking due account of the importance of the traditions and cultural values of each people for the protection and harmonious development of the child,

Recognising the importance of international co-operation for improving the living conditions of children in every country, in particular in the developing countries,

Have agreed as follows:

PART I

Article 1

For the purposes of the present Convention, a child means every human being below the age of eighteen years unless, under the law applicable to the child, majority is attained earlier.

Article 2

1. States Parties shall respect and ensure the rights set forth in the present Convention to each child within their jurisdiction without discrimination of any kind, irrespective of the child's or his or her parent's or legal guardian's race, colour, sex, language, religion, political or other opinion, national, ethnic or social origin, property, disability, birth or other status.

2. States Parties shall take all appropriate measures to ensure that the child is protected against all forms of discrimination or punishment on the basis of the status, activities, expressed opinions, or beliefs of the child's parents, legal guardians, or family members.

Article 3

1. In all actions concerning children, whether undertaken by public or private social welfare institutions, courts of law, administrative authorities or legislative bodies, the best interests of the child shall be a primary consideration.

2. States Parties undertake to ensure the child such protection and care as is necessary for his or her well-being, taking into account the rights and duties of his or her parents, legal guardians, or other individuals legally responsible for him or her, and, to this end, shall take all appropriate legislative and administrative measures.

3. States Parties shall ensure that the institutions, services and facilities responsible for the care or protection of children shall conform with the standards established by competent authorities, particularly in the areas of safety, health, in the number and suitability of their staff, as well as competent supervision.

Article 4

States Parties shall undertake all appropriate legislative, administrative, and other measures for the implementation of the rights recognised in the present Convention. With regard to economic, social and cultural rights, States Parties shall undertake such measures to the maximum extent of their available resources and, where needed, within the framework of international co-operation.

Article 5

States Parties shall respect the responsibilities, rights and duties of parents or, where applicable, the members of the extended family or community as provided for by local custom, legal guardians or other persons legally responsible for the child, to provide, in a manner consistent with the evolving capacities of the child, appropriate direction and guidance in the exercise by the child of the rights recognised in the present Convention.

Article 6

1. States Parties recognise that every child has the inherent right to life.

2. States Parties shall ensure to the maximum extent possible the survival and development of the child.

Article 7

1. The child shall be registered immediately after birth and shall have the right from birth to a name, the right to acquire a nationality and, as far as possible, the right to know and be cared for by his or her parents.

2. States Parties shall ensure the implementation of these rights in accordance with their national law and their obligations under the relevant international instruments in this field, in particular where the child would otherwise be stateless.

Article 8

1. States Parties undertake to respect the right of the child to preserve his or her identity, including nationality, name and family relations as recognised by law without unlawful interference.

2. Where a child is illegally deprived of some or all of the elements of his or her identity, States Parties shall provide appropriate assistance and protection, with a view to speedily re-establishing his or her identity.

Article 9

1. States Parties shall ensure that a child shall not be separated from his or her parents against their will, except when competent authorities subject to judicial review determine, in accordance with applicable law and procedures, that such separation is necessary for the best interests of the child. Such determination may be necessary in a particular case such as one involving abuse or neglect of the child by the parents, or one where the parents are living separately and a decision must be made as to the child's place of residence.

2. In any proceedings pursuant to paragraph I of the present Article, all interested parties shall be given an opportunity to participate in the proceedings and make their views known.

3. States Parties shall respect the right of the child who is separated from one or both parents to maintain personal relations and direct contact with both parents on a regular basis, except if it is contrary to the child's best interests.

4. Where such separation results from any action initiated by a State Party, such as the detention, imprisonment, exile, deportation or death (including death arising from any cause while the person is in the custody of the State) of one or both parents or of the child, that State Part shall, upon request, provide the parents, the child or, if appropriate, another member of the family with the essential information concerning the whereabouts of the absent member(s) of the family unless the provision of the information would be detrimental to the well-being of the child. States Parties shall further ensure that the submission of such a request shall of itself entail no adverse consequences for the person(s) concerned.

Article 10

1. In accordance with the obligation of States Parties under Article 9, paragraph I, applications by a child or his or her parents to enter or leave a State Party for the purpose of family reunification shall be dealt with by States Parties in a positive, humane and expeditious manner.

States Parties shall further ensure that the submission of such a request shall entail no adverse consequences for the applicants and for the members of their family.

2. A child whose parents reside in different States shall have the right to maintain on a regular basis, save in exceptional circumstances personal relations and direct contacts with both parents. Towards that end and in accordance with the obligation of States Parties under Article 9, paragraph 2, States Parties shall respect the right of the child and his or her parents to leave any country, including their own, and to enter their own country. The right to leave any country shall be subject only to such restrictions as are prescribed by law and which are necessary to protect the national security, public order (*ordre public*), public health or morals or the rights and freedoms of others and are consistent with the other rights recognised in the present Convention.

Article 11

1. States Parties shall take measures to combat the illicit transfer and non-return of children abroad.

2. To this end, States Parties shall promote the conclusion of bilateral or multilateral agreements or accession to existing agreements.

Article 12

1. States Parties shall assure to the child who is capable of forming his or her own views the right to express those views freely in all matters affecting the child, the views of the child being given due weight in accordance with the age of maturity of the child.

2. For this purpose, the child shall in particular be provided the opportunity to be heard in any judicial and administrative proceedings affecting the child, either directly, or through a representative or an appropriate body, in a manner consistent with the procedural rules of national law.

Article 13

1. The child shall have the right to freedom of expression; this right shall include freedom to seek, receive and impart information and ideas of all kinds, regardless of frontiers, either orally, in writing or in print, in the form of art, or through any other media of the child's choice.

2. The exercise of this right may be subject to certain restrictions, but these shall only be such as are provided by law and are necessary:

(a) For respect of the rights or reputations of others; or

(b) For the protection of national security or of public order (*ordre public*), or of public health or morals.

Article 14

1. States Parties shall respect the right of the child to freedom of thought, conscience and religion.

2. States Parties shall respect the rights and duties of the parents and, when applicable, legal guardians, to provide direction to the child in the exercise of his or her right in a manner consistent with the evolving capacities of the child.

3. Freedom to manifest one's religion or beliefs may be subject only to such limitations as are prescribed by law and are necessary to protect public safety, order, health or morals, or the fundamental rights and freedoms of others.

Article 15

1. States Parties recognise the rights of the child to freedom of association and to freedom of peaceful assembly.

2. No restrictions may be placed on the exercise of these rights other than those imposed in conformity with the law and which are necessary in a democratic society in the interests of national security or public safety, public order (*ordre public*), the protection of public health or morals or the protection of the rights and freedoms of others.

Article 16

1. No child shall be subjected to arbitrary or unlawful interference with his or her privacy, family, home or correspondence, nor to unlawful attacks on his or her honour and reputation.

2. The child has the right to the protection of the law against such interference or attacks.

Article 17

States Parties recognise the important function performed by the mass media and shall ensure that the child has access to information and material from a diversity of national and international sources, especially those aimed at the promotion of his or her social, spiritual and moral well-being and physical and mental health. To this end, States Parties shall:

(a) Encourage the mass media to disseminate information and material of social and cultural benefit to the child and in accordance with the spirit of Article 29;

(b) Encourage international co-operation in the production, exchange and dissemination of such information and material from a diversity of cultural, national and international sources;

(c) Encourage the production and dissemination of children's books;

(d) Encourage the mass media to have particular regard to the linguistic needs of the child who belongs to a minority group or who is indigenous;

(e) Encourage the development of appropriate guidelines for the protection of the child from information and material injurious to his or her well-being, bearing in mind the provisions of Articles 13 and 18.

Article 18

1. States Parties shall use their best efforts to ensure recognition of the principle that both parents have common responsibilities for the upbringing and development of the child. Parents or, as the case may be, legal guardians, have the primary responsibility for the upbringing and development of the child. The best interests of the child will be their basis concern.

2. For the purpose of guaranteeing and promoting the rights set forth in the present Convention, States Parties shall render appropriate assistance to parents and legal guardians in the performance of their child-rearing responsibilities and shall ensure the development of institutions, facilities and services for the care of children.

3. States Parties shall take all appropriate measures to ensure that children of working parents have the right to benefit from child-care services and facilities for which they are eligible.

Article 19

1. States Parties shall take all appropriate legislative, administrative, social and educational measures to protect the child from all forms of physical or mental violence, injury or abuse, neglect or negligent treatment, maltreatment or exploitation, including sexual abuse, while in the care of parent(s), legal guardian(s), or any other person who has the care of the child.

2. Such protective measures should, as appropriate, include effective procedures for the establishment of social programmes to provide necessary support for the child and for those who have the care of the child, as well as for other forms of prevention and for identification, reporting, referral, investigation, treatment and follow-up of instances of child maltreatment described heretofore, and, as appropriate, for judicial involvement.

Article 20

1. A child temporarily or permanently deprived of his or her family environment, or in whose own best interests cannot be allowed to remain in that environment, shall be entitled to special protection and assistance provided by the State.

2. States Parties shall in accordance with their national laws ensure alternative care for such a child.

3. Such care could include, *inter alia*, foster placement, *kafalah* of Islamic law, adoption or if necessary placement in suitable institutions for the care of children. When considering solutions, due regard shall be paid to the desirability of continuity in a child's upbringing and to the child's ethnic, religious, cultural and linguistic background.

Article 21

States Parties that recognise and/or permit the system of adoption shall ensure that the best interests of the child shall be the paramount consideration and they shall:

(a) Ensure that the adoption of a child is authorised only by competent authorities who determine, in accordance with applicable law and procedures and on the basis of all pertinent and reliable information, that the adoption is permissible in view of the child's status concerning parents, relatives and legal guardians and that, if required, the persons concerned have given their informed consent to the adoption on the basis of such counselling as may be necessary;

(b) Recognise that inter-country adoption may be considered as an alternative means of child's care, if the child cannot be placed in a foster or an adoptive family or cannot in any suitable manner be cared for in the child's country of origin;

(c) Ensure that the child concerned by inter-country adoption enjoys safeguards and standards equivalent to those existing in the case of national adoption;

(d) Take all appropriate measures to ensure that, in inter-country adoption, the placement does not result in improper financial gain for those involved in it;

(e) Promote, where appropriate, the objectives of the present article by concluding bilateral or multilateral arrangements or agreements, and endeavour, within this framework, to ensure that the placement of the child in another country is carried out by competent authorities or organs.

Article 22

1. States Parties shall take appropriate measures to ensure that a child who is seeking refugee status or who is considered a refugee in accordance with applicable international or domestic law and procedures shall, whether unaccompanied or accompanied by his or her parents or by any other person, receive appropriate protection and humanitarian assistance in the enjoyment of applicable rights set forth in the present Convention and in other international human rights or humanitarian instruments to which the said States are Parties.

2. For this purpose, States Parties shall provide, as they consider appropriate, co-operation in any efforts by the United Nations and other competent inter-governmental organisations or non-governmental organisations co-operating with the United Nations to protect and assist such a child and to trace the parents or other members of the family of any refugee child in order to obtain information necessary for reunification with his or her family. In cases where no parents or other members of the family can be found the child shall be accorded the same protection as any other child permanently or temporarily deprived of his or her family environment for any reason, as set forth in the present Convention.

Article 23

1. States Parties recognise that a mentally or physically disabled child should enjoy a full and decent life, in conditions which ensure dignity, promote self-reliance and facilitate the child's active participation in the community.

2. States Parties recognise the right of the disabled child to special care and shall encourage and ensure the extension, subject to available resources, to the eligible child and those responsible for his or her care, of assistance for which application is made and which is appropriate to the child's condition and to the circumstances of the parents or others caring for the child.

3. Recognising the special needs of a disabled child, assistance extended in accordance with paragraph 2 of the present article shall be provided free of charge, whenever possible, taking into account the financial resources of the parents or others caring for the child, and shall be designed to ensure that the disabled child has effective access to and receives education, training, health care services, rehabilitation services, preparation for employment and recreation opportunities in a manner conducive to the child's achieving the fullest possible social integration and individual development, including his or her cultural and spiritual development.

4. States Parties shall promote, in the spirit of international co-operation, the exchange of appropriate information in the field of preventive health care and of medical, psychological and functional treatment of disabled children, including dissemination of and access to information concerning methods of rehabilitation, education and vocational services, with the aim of enabling States Parties to improve their capabilities and skills and to widen their experience in these areas. In this regard, particular account shall be taken of the needs of developing countries.

Article 24

1. States Parties recognise the right of the child to the enjoyment of the highest attainable standard of health and to facilities for the treatment of illness and rehabilitation of health. States Parties shall

95

UWCC LIBRARY

strive to ensure that no child is deprived of his or her right of access to such health care services.

2. States Parties shall pursue full implementation of this right and, in particular, shall take appropriate measures:

(a) To diminish infant and child mortality;

(b) To ensure the provision of necessary medical assistance and health care to all children with emphasis on the development of primary health care;

(c) To combat disease and malnutrition, including within the framework of primary health care, through, *inter alia*, the application of readily available technology and through the provision of adequate nutritious foods and clean drinking-water, taking into consideration the dangers and risks of environmental pollution;

(d) To ensure appropriate pre-natal and post-natal health care for mothers;

(e) To ensure that all segments of society, in particular parents and children, are informed, have access to education and are supported in the use of basic knowledge of child health and nutrition, the advantages of breast-feeding, hygiene and environmental sanitation and the prevention of accidents;

(f) To develop preventive health care, guidance for parents and family planning education and services.

3. States Parties shall take all effective and appropriate measures with a view to abolishing traditional practices prejudicial to the health of children.

4. States Parties undertake to promote and encourage international co-operation with a view to achieving progressively the full realisation of the right recognised in the present article. In this regard, particular account shall be taken of the needs of developing countries.

Article 25

States Parties recognise the right of a child who has been placed by the competent authorities for the purposes of care, protection or treatment of his or her physical or mental health, to a periodic review of the treatment provided to the child and all other circumstances relevant to his or her placement.

Article 26

1. States Parties shall recognise for every child the right to benefit from social security, including social insurance, and shall take the necessary measures to achieve the full realisation of this right in accordance with their national law.

2. The benefits should, where appropriate, be granted, taking into account the resources and the circumstances of the child and persons having responsibility for the maintenance of the child, as well as any other consideration relevant to an application for benefits made by or on behalf of the child.

Article 27

1. States Parties recognise the right of every child to a standard of living adequate for the child's physical, mental, spiritual, moral and social development.

2. The parent(s) or others responsible for the child have the primary responsibility to secure, within their abilities and financial capacities, the conditions of living necessary for the child's development.

3. States Parties, in accordance with national conditions and within their means, shall take appropriate measures to assist parents and others responsible for the child to implement this right and shall in case of need provide material assistance and support programmes, particularly with regard to nutrition, clothing and housing.

4. States Parties shall take all appropriate measures to secure the recovery of maintenance for the child from the parents or other persons having financial responsibility for the child, both within the State Party and from abroad. In particular, where the person having financial responsibility for the child lives in a State different from that of the child, States Parties shall promote the accession to international agreements or the conclusion of such agreements, as well as the making of other appropriate arrangements.

Article 28

1. States Parties recognise the right of the child to education, and with a view to achieving this right progressively and on the basis of equal opportunity, they shall, in particular:

(a) Make primary education compulsory and available free to all;

(b) Encourage the development of different forms of secondary education, including general and vocational education, make them available and accessible to every child, and take appropriate measures such as the introduction of free education and offering financial assistance in case of need;

(c) Make higher education accessible to all on the basis of capacity by every appropriate means;

(d) Make educational and vocational information and guidance available and accessible to all children;

(e) Take measures to encourage regular attendance at schools and the reduction of drop-out rates.

2. States Parties shall take all appropriate measures to ensure that school discipline is administered in a manner consistent with the child's human dignity and in conformity with the present Convention.

3. States Parties shall promote and encourage international co-operation in matters relating to education, in particular with a view to contributing to the elimination of ignorance and illiteracy throughout the world and facilitating access to scientific and technical knowledge and modern teaching methods. In this regard, particular account shall be taken of the needs of developing countries.

Article 29

1. States Parties agree that the education of the child shall be directed to:

(a) The development of the child's personality, talents and mental and physical abilities to their fullest potential;

(b) The development of respect for human rights and fundamental freedoms, and for the principles enshrined in the Charter of the United Nations;

(c) The development of respect for the child's parents, his or her own cultural identity, language and values, for the national values of the country in which the child is living, the country from which he or she may originate, and for civilisations different from his or her own;

(d) The preparation of the child for responsible life in a free society, in the spirit of understanding, peace, tolerance, equality of sexes, and friendship among all peoples, ethnic, national and religious groups and persons of indigenous origin;

(e) The development of respect for the natural environment.

2. No part of the present Article or Article 28 shall be construed so as to interfere with the liberty of individuals and bodies to establish and direct educational institutions, subject always to the observance of the principles set forth in paragraph I of the present Article and to the requirements that the education given in such institutions shall conform to such minimum standards as may be laid down by the State.

Article 30

In those States in which ethnic, religious or linguistic minorities or persons of indigenous origin exist, a child belonging to such a minority or who is indigenous shall not be denied the right, in community with other members of his or her group, to enjoy his or her own culture, to profess and practise his or her own religion, or to use his or her own language.

Article 31

1. States Parties recognise the right of the child to rest and leisure, to engage in play and recreational activities appropriate to the age of the child and to participate freely in cultural life and the arts.

2. States Parties shall respect and promote the right of the child to participate full in cultural and artistic life and shall encourage the provision of appropriate and equal opportunities for cultural, artistic, recreational and leisure activity.

Article 32

1. States Parties recognise the right of the child to be protected from economic exploitation and from performing any work that is likely to be hazardous or to interfere with the child's education, or to be harmful to the child's health or physical, mental, spiritual, moral or social development.

2. States Parties shall take legislative, administrative, social and educational measures to ensure the implementation of the present article. To this end, and having regard to the relevant provisions of other international instruments, States Parties shall in particular:

(a) Provide for a minimum age or minimum ages for admission to employment;

(b) Provide for appropriate regulation of the hours and conditions of employment;

(c) Provide for appropriate penalties or other sanctions to ensure the effective enforcement of the present article.

Article 33

States Parties shall take all appropriate measures, including legislative, administrative, social and educational measures, to protect children from the illicit use of narcotic drugs and psychotropic substances as defined in the relevant international treaties, and to prevent the use of children in the illicit production and trafficking of such substances.

Article 34

States Parties undertake to protect the child from all forms of sexual exploitation and sexual abuse. For these purposes, States Parties shall in particular take all appropriate national, bilateral and multilateral measures to prevent:

(a) The inducement or coercion of a child to engage in any unlawful sexual activity;

(b) The exploitative use of children in prostitution or other unlawful sexual practices;

(c) The exploitative use of children in pornographic performances and materials.

Article 35

States Parties shall take all appropriate national, bilateral and multi-lateral measures to prevent the abduction of, the sale of or traffic in children for any purpose or in any form.

Article 36

States Parties shall protect the child against all other forms of exploitation prejudicial to any aspects of the child's welfare.

Article 37

States Parties shall ensure that:

(a) No child shall be subjected to torture or other cruel, inhuman or degrading treatment or punishment. Neither capital punishment nor life imprisonment without possibility of release shall be imposed for offences committed by persons below eighteen years of age;

(b) No child shall be deprived of his or her liberty unlawfully or arbitrarily. The arrest, detention or imprisonment of a child shall be in conformity with the law and shall be used only as a measure of last resort and for the shortest appropriate period of time;

(c) Every child deprived of liberty shall be treated with humanity and respect for the inherent dignity of the human person, and in a manner which takes into account the needs of persons of his or her age. In particular, every child deprived of liberty shall be separated from adults unless it is considered in the child's best interest not to do so and shall have the right to maintain contact with his or her family through correspondence and visits, save in exceptional circumstances;

(d) Every child deprived of his or her liberty shall have the right to prompt access to legal and other appropriate assistance, as well as the right to challenge the legality of the deprivation of his or her liberty before a court or other competent, independent and impartial authority, and to a prompt decision on any such action.

Article 38

1. States Parties undertake to respect and to ensure report for rules of international humanitarian law applicable to them in armed conflicts which are relevant to the child.

2. States Parties shall take all feasible measures to ensure that persons who have not attained the age of fifteen years do not take a direct part in hostilities.

3. States Parties shall refrain from recruiting any person who has not attained the age of fifteen years into their armed forces. In recruiting among those persons who have attained the age of fifteen years but who have not attained the age of eighteen years, States Parties shall endeavour to give priority to those who are oldest.

4. In accordance with their obligations under international humanitarian law to protect the civilian population in armed conflicts, States Parties shall take all feasible measures to ensure protection and care of children who are affected by an armed conflict.

Article 39

States Parties shall take all appropriate measures to promote physical and psychological recovery and social reintegration of a child victim of: any form of neglect, exploitation, or abuse; torture or any other form of cruel, inhuman or degrading treatment or punishment; or armed conflicts. Such recovery and reintegration shall take place in an environment which fosters the health, self-respect and dignity of the child.

Article 40

1. States Parties recognise the right of every child alleged as, accused of, or recognised as having infringed the penal law to be treated in a manner consistent with the promotion of the child's sense of dignity and worth, which reinforces the child's respect for the human rights and fundamental freedoms of others and which takes into account the child's age and the desirability of promoting the child's reintegration and the child's assuming a constructive role in society.

2. To this end, and having regard to the relevant provisions of international instruments, States Parties shall, in particular, ensure that:

(a) No child shall be alleged as, be accused of, or recognised as having infringed the penal law by reason of acts or omissions that were not prohibited by national or international law at the time they were committed;

(b) Every child alleged as or accused of having infringed the penal law has at least the following guarantees:

   (i) To be presumed innocent until proven guilty according to law;

   (ii) To be informed promptly and directly of the charges against him or her, and, if appropriate, through his or her parents or legal guardians, and to have legal or other appropriate assistance in the preparation and presentation of his or her defence;

   (iii) To have the matter determined without delay by a competent, independent and impartial authority or judicial body in a fair hearing according to law, in the presence of legal or other appropriate assistance and, unless it is considered not to be in the best interest of the child, in particular, taking into account his or her age or situation, his or her parents or legal guardians;

(iv) Not to be compelled to give testimony or to confess guilt; to examine or have examined adverse witnesses and to obtain the participation and examination of witnesses on his or her behalf under conditions of equality;

(v) If considered to have infringed the penal law, to have this decision and any measures imposed in consequence thereof reviewed by a higher competent, independent and impartial authority or judicial body according to law;

(vi) To have the free assistance of an interpreter if the child cannot understand or speak the language used;

(vii) To have his or her privacy fully respected at all stages of the proceedings.

3. States Parties shall seek to promote the establishment of laws, procedures, authorities and institutions specifically applicable to children alleged as, accused of, or recognised as having infringed the penal law, and, in particular:

(a) The establishment of a minimum age below which children shall be presumed not to have the capacity to infringe the penal law;

(b) Whenever appropriate and desirable, measures for dealing with such children without resorting to judicial proceedings, providing that human rights and legal safeguards are fully respected.

4. A variety of dispositions, such as care, guidance and supervision orders; counselling; probation; foster care; education and vocational training programmes and other alternatives to institutional care shall be available to ensure that children are dealt with in a manner appropriate to their well-being and proportionate both to their circumstances and the offence.

Article 41

Nothing in the present Convention shall affect any provisions which are more conducive to the realisation of the rights of the child and which may be contained in:

(a) The law of a State Party; or

(b) International law in force for that State.

PART II

Article 42

States Parties undertake to make the principles and provisions of the Convention widely known, by appropriate and active means, to adults and children alike.

Article 43

1. For the purpose of examining the progress made by States Parties in achieving the realisation of the obligations undertaken in the present Convention, there shall be established a Committee on the Rights of the Child, which shall carry out the functions hereinafter provided.

2. The Committee shall consist of ten experts of high moral standing and recognised competence in the field covered by this Convention. The members of the Committee shall be elected by States Parties from among their nationals and shall serve in the personal capacity, consideration being given to equitable geographical distribution, as well as to the principal legal systems.

3. The members of the Committee shall be elected by secret ballot from a list of persons nominated by States Parties. Each State Party may nominate one person from among its own nationals.

4. The initial election to the Committee shall be held no later than six months after the date of the entry into force of the present Convention and thereafter every second year. At least four months before the date of each election, the Secretary-General of the United Nations shall address a letter to State Parties inviting them to submit their nominations within two months. The Secretary-General shall subsequently prepare a list in alphabetical order of all persons thus nominated, indicating States Parties which have nominated them, and shall submit it to the States Parties to the present Convention.

5. The elections shall be held at meetings of States Parties convened by the Secretary-General at United Nations Headquarters. At those meetings, for which two thirds of States Parties shall constitute a quorum, the persons elected to the Committee shall be those who obtain the largest number of votes and an absolute majority of the votes of the representatives of States Parties present and voting.

6. The members of the Committee shall be elected for a term of four years. They shall be eligible for re-election if renominated. The term of five of the members elected at the first election shall expire at the end of two years; immediately after the first election, the names of these five members shall be chosen by lot by the Chairman of the meeting.

7. If a member of the Committee dies or resigns or declares that for any other cause he or she can no longer perform the duties of the Committee, the State Party which nominated the member shall appoint another expert from among its nationals to serve for the remainder of the term, subject to the approval of the Committee.

8. The Committee shall establish its own rules of procedure.

9. The Committee shall elect its officers for a period of two years.

10. The meetings of the Committee shall normally be held at United Nations Headquarters or at any other convenient place as determined by the Committee. The Committee shall normally meet annually. The duration of the meetings of the Committee shall be determined, and reviewed, if necessary, by a meeting of the States Parties to the present Convention, subject to the approval of the General Assembly.

11. The Secretary-General of the United Nations shall provide the necessary staff and facilities for the effective performance of the functions of the Committee under the present Convention.

12. With the approval of the General Assembly, the members of the Committee established under the present Convention shall receive emoluments from United Nations resources on such terms and conditions as the Assembly may decide.

Article 44

1. States Parties undertake to submit to the Committee, through the Secretary-General of the United Nations, reports on the measures they have adopted which give effect to the rights recognised herein and on the progress made on the enjoyment of those rights:

(a) Within two years of the entry into force of the Convention for the State Party concerned;

(b) Thereafter every five years.

2. Reports made under the present Article shall indicate factors and difficulties, if any, affecting the degree of fulfilment of the obligations under the present Convention. Reports shall also contain sufficient information to provide the Committee with a comprehensive understanding of the implementation of the Convention in the country concerned.

3. A State Party which has submitted a comprehensive initial report to the Committee need not, in its subsequent reports submitted in accordance with paragraph I *(b)* of the present Article, repeat basic information previously provided.

4. The Committee may request from States Parties further information relevant to the implementation of the Convention.

5. The Committee shall submit to the General Assembly, through the Economic and Social Council, every two years, reports on its activities.

6. States Parties shall make their reports widely available to the public in their own countries.

Article 45

In order to foster the effective implementation of the Convention and to encourage international co-operation in the field covered by the Convention:

(a) The specialised agencies, the United Nations Children's Fund, and other United Nations organs shall be entitled to be represented at the consideration of the implementation of such provisions of the present Convention as fall within the scope of their mandate. The Committee may invite the specialised agencies, the United Nations Children's Fund and other competent bodies as it may consider appropriate to provide expert advice on the implementation of the Convention in areas falling within the scope of their respective mandates. The Committee may invite the specialised agencies, the United Nations Children's Fund, and other United Nations organs to submit reports on the implementation of the Convention in areas falling within the scope of their activities;

(b) The Committee shall transmit, as it may consider appropriate, to the specialised agencies, the United nations Children's Fund and other competent bodies, any reports from States Parties that contain a request, or indicate a need, for technical advice or assistance, along with the Committee's observations and suggestions, if any, on these requests or indications;

(c) The Committee may recommend to the General Assembly to request the Secretary-General to undertake on its behalf studies on specific issues relating to the rights of the child;

(d) The Committee may make suggestions and general recommendations based on information received pursuant to Articles 44 and 45 of the present Convention. Such suggestions and general recommendations shall be transmitted to any State Party concerned and reported to the General Assembly, together with comments, if any, from States Parties.

PART III

Article 46

The present Convention shall be open for signature by all States.

Article 47

The present Convention is subject to ratification. Instruments of ratification shall be deposited with the Secretary-General of the United Nations.

Article 48

The present Convention shall remain open for accession by any States. The instruments of accession shall be deposited with the Secretary-General of the United Nations.

Article 49

1. The present Convention shall enter into force on the thirtieth day following the date of deposit with the Secretary-General of the United Nations of the twentieth instrument of ratification or accession.

2. For each State ratifying or acceding to the Convention after the deposit of the twentieth instrument of ratification or accession, the Convention shall enter into force on the thirtieth day after the deposit by such State of its instrument of ratification or accession.

Article 50

1. Any State Party may propose an amendment and file it with the Secretary-General of the United Nations. The Secretary-General shall thereupon communicate the proposed amendment to States Parties, with a request that they indicate whether they favour a conference of States Parties for the purpose of considering and voting upon the proposals. In the event that, within four months from the date of such communication, at least one third of the States Parties favour such a conference, the Secretary-General shall convene the conference under the auspices of the United Nations. Any amendment adopted by a majority of States Parties present and voting at the conference shall be submitted to the General Assembly for approval.

2. An amendment adopted in accordance with paragraph I of the present article shall enter into force when it has been approved by the General Assembly of the United Nations and accepted by a two-thirds majority of States Parties.

3. When an amendment enters into force, it shall be binding on those States Parties which have accepted it, other States Parties still being bound by the provisions of the present Convention and any earlier amendments which they have accepted.

Article 51

1. The Secretary-General of the United Nations shall receive and circulate to all States the text of reservations made by States at the time of ratification or accession.

2. A reservation incompatible with the object and purpose of the present Convention shall not be permitted.

3. Reservations may be withdrawn at any time by notification to that effect addressed to the Secretary-General of the United Nations, who shall then inform all States. Such notification shall take effect on the date on which it is received by the Secretary-General.

Article 52

At State Party may denounce the present Convention by written notification to the Secretary-General of the United Nations. Denunciation becomes effective one year after the date of receipt of the notification by the Secretary-General.

Article 53

The Secretary-General of the United Nations is designated as the depositary of the present Convention.

Article 54

The original of the present Convention, of which the Arabic, Chinese, English, French, Russian and Spanish texts are equally authentic, shall be deposited with the Secretary-General of the United Nations.

In witness thereof the undersigned plenipotentiaries, being duly authorised thereto by their respective Governments, have signed the present Convention.

F. UNITED NATIONS DECLARATION ON SOCIAL AND LEGAL PRINCIPLES RELATING TO THE PROTECTION AND WELFARE OF CHILDREN, WITH SPECIAL REFERENCE TO FOSTER PLACEMENT AND ADOPTION NATIONALLY AND INTERNATIONALLY 1986

THE GENERAL ASSEMBLY,

Recalling the Universal Declaration of Human Rights, the International Covenant on Economic, Social and Cultural Rights, the International Covenant on Civil and Political Rights, the International Convention on the Elimination of All Forms of Racial Discrimination and the Convention on the Elimination of All Forms of Discrimination against Women,

Recalling also the Declaration of the Rights of the Child, which it proclaimed by its resolution 1386 (XIV) of 20 November 1959,

Reaffirming principle 6 of that Declaration, which states that the child shall, wherever possible, grow up in the care and under the responsibility of his parents and, in any case, in an atmosphere of affection and of moral and material security,

Concerned at the large number of children who are abandoned or become orphans owing to violence, internal disturbance, armed conflicts, natural disasters, economic crises or social problems,

Bearing in mind that in all foster placement and adoption procedures the best interests of the child should be the paramount consideration,

Recognising that under the principal legal systems of the world, various valuable alternative institutions exist, such as the Kafala of Islamic Law, which provide substitute care to children who cannot be cared for by their own parents,

Recognising further that only where a particular institution is recognised and regulated by the domestic law of State would the provisions of this Declaration relating to that institution be relevant and that such provisions would in no way affect the existing alternative institutions in other legal systems,

Conscious of the need to proclaim universal principles to be taken into account in cases where procedures are instituted relating to foster placement or adoption of a child, either nationally or internationally,

Bearing in mind, however, that the principles set forth hereunder do not impose on States such legal institutions as foster placement or adoption,

Proclaims the following principles:

A. General Family and Child Welfare

Article 1

Every State should give a high priority to family and child welfare.

Article 2

Child welfare depends upon good family welfare.

Article 3

The first priority for a child is to be cared for by his or her own parents.

Article 4

When care by the child's own parents is unavailable or inappropriate, care by relatives of the child's parents, by another substitute — foster or adoptive — family or, if necessary, by an appropriate institution should be considered.

Article 5

In all matters relating to the placement of a child outside the care of the child's own parents, the best interests of the child, particularly his or her need for affection and right to security and continuing care, should be the paramount consideration.

Article 6

Persons responsible for foster placement or adoption procedures should have professional or other appropriate training.

Article 7

Governments should determine the adequacy of their national child welfare services and consider appropriate actions.

Article 8

The child should at all times have a name, a nationality and a legal representative. The child should not, as a result of foster placement, adoption or any alternative regime, be deprived of his or her name, nationality or legal representative unless the child thereby acquires a new name, nationality or legal representative.

Article 9

The need of a foster or an adopted child to know about his or her background should be recognised by persons responsible for the child's care unless this is contrary to the child's best interests.

B. FOSTER PLACEMENT

Article 10

Foster placement of children should be regulated by law.

Article 11

Foster family care, though temporary in nature, may continue, if necessary, until adulthood but should not preclude either prior return to the child's own parents or adoption.

Article 12

In all matters of foster family care, the prospective foster parents and, as appropriate, the child and his or her own parents should be properly involved. A competent authority or agency should be responsible for supervision to ensure the welfare of the child.

C. ADOPTION

Article 13

The primary aim of adoption is to provide the child who cannot be cared for by his or her own parents with a permanent family.

Article 14

In considering possible adoption placements, persons responsible for them should select the most appropriate environment for the child.

Article 15

Sufficient time and adequate counselling should be given to the child's own parents, the prospective adoptive parents and, as appropriate, the child in order to reach a decision on the child's future as early as possible.

Article 16

The relationship between the child to be adopted and the prospective adoptive parents should be observed by child welfare agencies or services prior to the adoption. Legislation should ensure that the child is recognised in law as a member of the adoptive family and enjoys all the rights pertinent thereto.

Article 17

If a child cannot be placed in a foster or an adoptive family or cannot in any suitable manner be cared for in the country of origin, intercountry adoption may be considered as an alternative means of providing the child with a family.

Article 18

Governments should establish policy, legislation and effective supervision for the protection of children involved in intercountry adoption. Intercountry adoption should, wherever possible, only be undertaken when such measures have been established in the States concerned.

Article 19

Policies should be established and laws enacted, where necessary, for the prohibition of abduction and of any other act for illicit placement of children.

Article 20

In intercountry adoption, placements should, as a rule, be made through competent authorities or agencies with application of safeguards and standards equivalent to those existing in respect of national adoption. In no case should the placement result in improper financial gain for those involved in it.

Article 21

In intercountry adoption through persons acting as agents for prospective adoptive parents, special precautions should be taken in order to protect the child's legal and social interests.

Article 22

No intercountry adoption should be considered before it has been established that the child is legally free for adoption and that any pertinent documents necessary to complete the adoption, such as the consent of competent authorities, will become available. It must also be established that the child will be able to migrate and to join the prospective adoptive parents and may obtain their nationality.

Article 23

In intercountry adoption, as a rule, the legal validity of the adoption should be assured in each of the countries involved.

Article 24

Where the nationality of the child differs from that of the prospective adoptive parents, all due weight shall be given to both the law of the State of which the child is a national and the law of the State of which the prospective adoptive parents are nationals. In this connection due regard shall be given to the child's cultural and religious background and interests.

G. EUROPEAN CONVENTION ON THE ADOPTION OF CHILDREN 1967

The member States of the Council of Europe, signatory hereto,

Considering that the aim of the Council of Europe is to achieve a greater unity between its Members for the purpose, among others, of facilitating their social progress;

Considering that, although the institution of the adoption of children exists in all member countries of the Council of Europe, there are in those countries differing views as to the principles which should govern adoptions and differences in the procedure for effecting, and the legal consequences of, adoption; and

Considering that the acceptance of common principles and practices with respect to the adoption of children would help to reduce the difficulties caused by those differences and at the same time promote the welfare of children who are adopted,

Have agreed as follows:

PART I

Undertakings and Field of Application

Article 1

Each Contracting Party undertakes to ensure the conformity of its law with the provisions of Part II of this Convention and to notify the Secretary General of the Council of Europe of the measures taken for that purpose.

Article 2

Each Contracting Party undertakes to give consideration to the provisions set out in Part III of this Convention, and if it gives effect, or if, having given effect, it ceases to give effect to any of these provisions, it shall notify the Secretary General of the Council of Europe.

Article 3

This Convention applies only to legal adoption of a child who, at the time when the adopter applies to adopt him, has not attained the age of 18, is not and has not been married, and is not deemed in law to have come of age.

Part II

Essential Provisions

Article 4

An adoption shall be valid only if it is granted by a judicial or administrative authority (hereinafter referred to as "the competent authority").

Article 5

1. Subject to paragraphs 2 to 4 of this Article, an adoption shall not be granted unless at least the following consent to the adoption have been given and not withdrawn:

(a) the consent of the mother and, where the child is legitimate, the father; or if there is neither father nor mother to consent, the consent of any person or body who may be entitled in their place to exercise their parental rights in that respect;

(b) the consent of the spouse of the adopter.

2. The competent authority shall not:

(a) dispense with the consent of any person mentioned in paragraph 1 of this Article, or

(b) overrule the refusal to consent of any person or body mentioned in the said paragraph 1,

save on exceptional grounds determined by law.

3. If the father or mother is deprived of his or her parental rights in respect of the child, or at least of the right to consent to an adoption, the law may provide that it shall not be necessary to obtain his or her consent.

4. A mother's consent to the adoption of her child shall not be accepted unless it is given at such time after the birth of the child, not being less than six weeks, as may be prescribed by law, or, if no such time has been prescribed, at such time as, in the opinion of the competent authority, will have enabled her to recover sufficiently from the effects of giving birth to the child.

5. For the purposes of this Article "father" and "mother" mean the persons who are according to law the parents of the child.

Article 6

1. The law shall not permit a child to be adopted except by either two persons married to each other, whether they adopt simultaneously or successively, or by one person.

2. The law shall not permit a child to be again adopted save in one or more of the following circumstances:

(a) where the child is adopted by the spouse of the adopter,

(b) where the former adopter has died;

(c) where the former adoption has been annulled;

(d) where the former adoption has come to an end.

Article 7

1. A child may be adopted only if the adopter has attained the minimum age prescribed for the purpose, this age being neither less than 21 nor more than 35 years.

2. The law may, however, permit the requirement as to the minimum age to be waived:

(a) when the adopter is the child's father or mother, or

(b) by reason of exceptional circumstances.

Article 8

1. The competent authority shall not grant an adoption unless it is satisfied that the adoption will be in the interests of the child.

2. In each case the competent authority shall pay particular attention to the importance of the adoption providing the child with a stable and harmonious home.

3. As a general rule, the competent authority shall not be satisfied as aforesaid if the difference in age between the adopter and the child is less than the normal difference in age between parents and their children.

Article 9

1. The competent authority shall not grant an adoption until appropriate enquiries have been made concerning the adopter, the child and his family.

2. The enquiries, to the extent appropriate in each case, shall concern, *inter alia,* the following matters:

(a) the personality, health and means of the adopter, particulars of his home and household and his ability to bring up the child;

(b) why the adopter wishes to adopt the child;

(c) where only one of two spouses of the same marriage applies to adopt a child, why the other spouse does not join in the application;

(d) the mutual suitability of the child and the adopter, and the length of time that the child has been in his care and possession;

(e) the personality and health of the child, and subject to any limitations imposed by law, his antecedents;

(f) the views of the child with respect of the proposed adoption;

(g) the religious persuasion, if any, of the adopter and of the child.

3. These enquiries shall be entrusted to a person or body recognised for that purpose by law or by a judicial or administrative body. They shall, as far as practicable, be made by social workers who are qualified in this field as a result of either their training or their experience.

4. The provisions of this Article shall not affect the power or duty of the competent authority to obtain any information or evidence, whether or not within the scope of these enquiries, which it considers likely to be of assistance.

Article 10

1. Adoption confers on the adopter in respect of the adopted person the rights and obligations of every kind that a father or mother has in respect of a child born in lawful wedlock.

Adoption confers on the adopted person in respect of the adopter the rights and obligations of every kind that a child born in lawful wedlock has in respect of his father or mother.

2. When the rights and obligations referred to in paragraph 1 of this Article are created, any rights and obligations of the same kind existing between the adopted person and his father or mother or any other person or body shall cease to exist. Nevertheless, the law may provide that the spouse of the adopter retains his rights and obligations in respect of the adopted person if the latter is his legitimate, illegitimate or adopted child.

In addition the law may preserve the obligation of the parents to maintain (in the sense of *l'obligation d'entretenir* and *l'obligation alimentaire*) or set up in life or provide a dowry for the adopted person if the adopter does not discharge any such obligation.

3. As a general rule, means shall be provided to enable the adopted person to acquire the surname of the adopter either in substitution for, or in addition to, his own.

4. If the parent of a child born in lawful wedlock has a right to the enjoyment of that child's property, the adopter's right to the enjoyment of the adopted person's property may, notwithstanding paragraph 1 of this Article, be restricted by law.

5. In matters of succession, in so far as the law of succession gives a child born in lawful wedlock a right to share in the estate of his father or mother, an adopted child shall, for the like purposes, be treated as if he were a child of the adopter born in lawful wedlock.

Article 11

1. Where the adopted child does not have, in the case of an adoption by one person, the same nationality as the adopter, or in the case of an adoption by a married couple, their common nationality, the Contracting Party of which the adopter or adopters are nationals shall facilitate acquisition of its nationality by the child.

2. A loss of nationality which could result from an adoption shall be conditional upon possession or acquisition of another nationality.

Article 12

1. The number of children who may be adopted by an adopter shall not be restricted by law.

2. A person who has, or is able to have, a child born in lawful wedlock, shall not on that account be prohibited by law from adopting a child.

3. If adoption improves the legal position of a child, a person shall not be prohibited by law from adopting his own child not born in lawful wedlock.

Article 13

1. Before an adopted person comes of age the adoption may be revoked only by a decision of a judicial or administrative authority on serious grounds, and only if revocation on that ground is permitted by law.

2. The preceding paragraph shall not affect the case of:

(a) an adoption which is null and void;

(b) an adoption coming to an end where the adopted person becomes the legitimated child of the adopter.

Article 14

When the enquiries made pursuant to Articles 8 and 9 of this Convention relate to a person who lives or has lived in the territory of another Contracting Party, that Contracting Party shall, if a request for information is made, promptly endeavour to secure that the information requested is provided. The authorities may communicate directly with each other for this purpose.

Article 15

Provision shall be made to prohibit any improper financial advantage arising from a child being given up for adoption.

Article 16

Each Contracting Party shall retain the option of adopting provisions more favourable to the adopted child.

PART III

Supplementary Provisions

Article 17

An adoption shall not be granted until the child has been in the care of the adopters for a period long enough to enable a reasonable estimate to be made by the competent authority as to their future relations if the adoption were granted.

Article 18

The public authorities shall ensure the promotion and proper functioning of public or private agencies to which those who wish to adopt a child or to cause a child to be adopted may go for help and advice.

Article 19

The social and legal aspects of adoption shall be included in the curriculum for the training of social workers.

Article 20

1. Provision shall be made to enable an adoption to be completed without disclosing to the child's family the identity of the adopter.

2. Provisions shall be made to require or permit adoption proceedings to take place *in camera*.

3. The adopter and the adopted person shall be able to obtain a document which contains extracts from the public records arresting the fact, date and place of birth of the adopted person, but not expressly revealing the fact of adoption or the identity of this former parents.

4. Public records shall be kept and, in any event, their consents reproduced in such a way as to prevent persons who do not have a legitimate interest from learning the fact that a person has been adopted or, if that, is disclosed, the identity of his former parents.

PART IV

Final Clauses

Article 21

1. This Convention shall be open to signature by the member States of the Council of Europe. It shall be subject to ratification or acceptance. Instruments of ratification or acceptance shall be deposited with the Secretary General of the Council of Europe.

2. This Convention shall enter into force three months after the date of the deposit of the third instrument of ratification or acceptance.

3. In respect of a signatory State ratifying or accepting subsequently, the Convention shall come into force three months after the date of the deposit of its instrument of ratification or acceptance.

Article 22

1. After the entry into force of this Convention, the Committee of Ministers of the Council of Europe may invite any non-members State to accede thereto.

2. Such accession shall be effected by depositing with the Secretary General of the Council of Europe an instrument of accession which shall take effect three months after the date of its deposit.

H. AGREEMENT ON THE WORKING ARRANGEMENTS FOR THE CO-ORDINATION OF INTERCOUNTRY ADOPTION BETWEEN THE ROMANIAN COMMITTEE FOR ADOPTIONS AND THE UNITED KINGDOM 1992

Introduction

1. This Agreement is not a legal document but has been prepared to reflect current legislation governing the adoption of children in Romania and within the United Kingdom.

2. The Agreement is the basis for a working arrangement between the countries of the United Kingdom and the Romanian Committee for Adoptions concerning the processing of applications from those domiciled in the UK to adopt children from Romania who have been identified as being available for adoption by the Romanian Committee for Adoptions.

3. The Department of Health in England will act as agent for the Health Departments of Scotland, Wales and Northern Ireland in processing applications from prospective adopters.

General Principles

4. The guiding principles for this working arrangement are those set out in the United Nations Convention on the Rights of the Child, adopted by the General Assembly on 20 November, 1989.

5. These principles recognise that:

(a) intercountry adoption may be considered as an alternative means of child care if the child cannot be placed with foster parents or with an adoptive family or cared for in a suitable manner in the child's country of origin;

(b) in all actions concerning children, the best interests of the child shall be a primary consideration;

(c) the child who is the subject of intercountry adoption should enjoy safeguards and standards equivalent to those existing in the case of a national adoption;

(d) the placement of a child should be arranged by competent authorities in Romania and the United Kingdom;

(e) subject to paragraph 'f' below, no payment shall be made in relation to arrangements for adoptions;

(f) bona fide payments in respect of expenses and fees may be made.

Guidelines

6. Intercountry adoption of Romanian children must be performed according to Romanian and United Kingdom laws governing adoption.

7. The Department of Health will only forward applications for the adoption of Romanian children on behalf of those domiciled in the United Kingdom and received from the relevant local authority for the area in which the applicants live.

8. In respect of developing detailed procedures and requirements for the adoption of Romanian children, the Department of Health will co-operate exclusively with the Romanian Committee for Adoptions which is the authorised body in Romania responsible for identifying and listing children who may be available for adoption by people living abroad.

9. The Romanian Committee for Adoptions will accept only from the Department of Health applications for the adoption of Romanian children from those domiciled in the UK, including Romanian citizens domiciled in the United Kingdom.

10. The Department of Health and the Romanian Committee for Adoptions will develop detailed procedures and requirements for the adoption of Romanian children by those domiciled in the United Kingdom and Romanian citizens domiciled in the United Kingdom. These procedures shall include those specified in the Annex to this document which is to be regarded as an integral part of the Agreement.

Amendment Provision

11. The working arrangements may be amended at any time with the approval in writing of both parties. Either the Department of Health or the Romanian Committee for Adoptions may terminate the Agreement by giving three months notice in writing. Termination of the Agreement will not affect the completion of adoptions procedures already in progress at the time termination is to take effect.

ANNEX

PROCEDURES AND REQUIREMENTS FOR THE ADOPTION OF ROMANIAN CHILDREN

Eligible Applicants

12. Eligible applicants will:

(a) be couples married to each other for at least 3 years. Exceptionally, couples married less than 3 years and single people may be considered in respect of children with special needs or children over 10 years of age.

(b) The age ratio of adopting parents to children has been raised. The woman should should be no more than 40 years older than the child to be adopted and the man no more than 45 years older. (This brings the age ratios into line with those which already apply to prospective adopters seeking to adopt children with special needs.)
Also, the Committee are prepared to consider adoption applications for "special needs" children from prospective adopters who exceed the prescribed age ratio but whom the Department of Health is prepared to support.

(c) have no more than 2 children.

Eligible Children

13. Eligible children are those who are registered with the Romanian Committee for Adoptions who could not be entrusted or adopted in Romania within at least 6 months from their date of registration.

PROCEDURES

A. Application

14. An application to adopt a Romanian child will include the following documents which will be forwarded to the Romanian Committee for Adoptions by the Department of Health:

(a) a statement from the applicants expressing their desire to adopt a Romanian child. (This statement can be incorporated in the home study report.)

(b) copies of birth and marriage certificates;

(c) police statement of enquiries made, providing details (if any) of criminal convictions recorded in respect of each applicant;

(d) full reports on the health of applicants and comments on the health of other members of their household;

(e) statement of family income; (This statement can be incorporated in the home study report.)

(f) recent colour photographs of applicants and of any children born to the applicants or living in the applicant's household;

(g) home study reports prepared by the local authority in whose area the applicant lives. The report should include reference to:—
   — the applicant's motivation for adoption;
   — psychosocial history;
   — family dynamics;
   — attitude of children in the household towards the possible adoption;
   — knowledge of and attitudes towards Romanian culture;
   — attitudes of the immediate community;
   — other information of interest (eg religion).

The home study should also include a statement from the local authority in whose area the applicant lives indicating their opinion regarding the capability of the applicants to adopt a Romanian child, confirming that the applicants may adopt in accordance with the relevant domestic law in the United Kingdom. This statement is to be provided by the head of the adoption agency on letter-headed paper of the agency.

All documents must be certified by a solicitor registered in the United Kingdom as a true copy of the original documents and translated into Romanian.

B. Child Referral

15. The Romanian Committee for Adoptions will review applications and register the applicants on their waiting list. As children become available for adoption the Committee will select the family they deem most appropriate for the child and forward the following documents to the Department of Health:

(i) child's social case history including the circumstances surrounding his/her becoming available for adoption, having regard to the wishes and feelings of the child, taking into account the child's age and understanding;

(ii) child's medical history and current health status;

(iii) recent photograph of the child;

(iv) social and medical history of the child's birth parents, if available.

(v) child's certificate of birth;

(vi) notarised statement from the birth parents, or from the person having parental responsibility for the child, that consent for the child to be adopted has been freely given.

C. Child Acceptance

16. If the child identified for the prospective adopters is accepted, the couple will be asked to sign a 'Declaration of Intent to Adopt' which must be forwarded to the Romanian Committee for Adoptions by the Department of Health within 60 days of its receipt in the Department.

Exceptionally, the Department of Health will make representation to the Romanian Committee for Adoptions to extend the period of 60 days.

17. The Romanian Committee for Adoptions will be provided with follow-up reports for 2 years following the child's entry into the United Kingdom, describing the adjustment of the child into the family. These reports will be prepared by social workers approved by the local authority at regular intervals up to the time the adoption order is made in the United Kingdom.

The provision thereafter of follow-up reports for the remainder of the 2 years will be by agreement of the applicants and the Romanian Committee for Adoptions. These reports will be forwarded to the Romanian Committee for Adoptions by the Department of Health.

18. The applicants will travel to Romania within 30 days from the date of signing the 'Declaration of Intent to Adopt' in order to complete the adoption process in Romania.

19. If the child matched to the adopters is not accepted, the Romanian Committee for Adoptions will not offer that couple a second choice. The local authority will set out for the Committee the reasons why the child has not been accepted.

D. Other Provisions

20. The Romanian Committee for Adoptions will provide the applicants or their legal representatives with confirmation that the child could not be entrusted or adopted in Romania within at least 6 months from the date of his/her registration, as well as the file containing the documents regarding the applicants, referred to in section 15 of this Annex.

21. Applicants wishing to retain the services of a lawyer should make enquiries of the Romanian Bar Association in the district in which the child is resident.

22. In the event of a breakdown of the adoption placement or abandonment of the child in the UK, the local authority for the area in which the child resides is responsible for providing for the protection or placement of the child in accordance with the relevant domestic law in the United Kingdom.

23. The Department of Health is obliged to bring to the notice of the Romanian Committee for Adoptions all cases of breakdown of adoption placements in the United Kingdom involving a Romanian child which come to its attention.

Appendix 2

U.K. STATUTORY MATERIAL

A. ADOPTION ACT 1976, SS. 50–72 AND SCHED. 1, PARAS. 3-6

PART V

Registration and Revocation of Adoption Orders and Convention Adoptions

Adopted Children Register

50.—(1) The Registrar General shall maintain at the General Register Office a register, to be called the Adopted Children Register, in which shall be made such entries as may be directed to be made therein by adoption orders, but no other entries.

(2) A certified copy of an entry in the Adopted Children Register, if purporting to be sealed or stamped with the seal of the General Register Office, shall, without any further or other proof of that entry, be received as evidence of the adoption to which it relates and, where the entry contains a record of the date of the birth or the country or the district and sub-district of the birth of the adopted person, shall also be received as aforesaid as evidence of that date or country or district and sub-district in all respects as if the copy were a certified copy of an entry in the Registers of Births.

(3) The Registrar General shall cause an index of the Adopted Children Register to be made and kept in the General Register Office; and every person shall be entitled to search that index and to have a certified copy of any entry in the Adopted Children Register in all respects upon and subject to the same terms, conditions and regulations as to payment of fees and otherwise as are applicable under the Births and Deaths Registration Act 1953, and the Registration Service Act 1953, in respect of searches in other indexes kept in the General Register Office and in respect of the supply from that office of certified copies of entries in the certified copies of the Registers of Births and Deaths.

(4) The Registrar General shall, in addition to the Adopted Children Register and the index thereof, keep such other registers and books, and make such entries therein, as may be necessary to record and make traceable the connection between any entry in the Registers of Births which has been marked "Adopted" and any corresponding entry in the Adopted Children Register.

(5) The registers and books kept under subsection (4) shall not be, nor shall any index thereof be, open to public inspection or search, and the Registrar General shall not furnish any person with any

information contained in or with any copy or extract from any such registers or books except in accordance with section 51 or under an order of any of the following courts, that is to say—

(a) the High Court;

(b) the Westminster County Court or such other county court as may be prescribed; and

(c) the court by which an adoption order was made in respect of the person to whom the information, copy or extract relates.

(6) In relation to an adoption order made by a magistrates' court, the reference in paragraph (c) of subsection (5) to the court by which the order was made includes a reference to a court acting for the same petty sessions area.

(7) Schedule 1 to this Act, which, among other things, provides for the registration of adoptions and the amendment of adoption orders, shall have effect.

Disclosure of Birth Records of Adopted Children

51.—(1) Subject to what follows, the Registrar General shall on an application made in the prescribed manner by an adopted person a record of whose birth is kept by the Registrar General and who has attained the age of 18 years supply to that person on payment of the prescribed fee (if any) such information as is necessary to enable that person to obtain a certified copy of the record of his birth.

(2) On an application made in the prescribed manner by an adopted person under the age of 18 years, a record of whose birth is kept by the Registrar General and who is intending to be married in England or Wales, and on payment of the prescribed fee (if any), the Registrar General shall inform the applicant whether or not it appears from information contained in the registers of live births or other records that the applicant and the person whom he intends to marry may be within the prohibited degrees of relationship for the purposes of the Marriage Act 1949.

(3) Before supplying any information to an applicant under subsection (1), the Registrar General shall inform the applicant that counselling services are available to him—

(a) if he is in England and Wales—

(i) at the General Register Office;

(ii) from the local authority in whose area he is living;

(iii) where the adoption order relating to him was made in England and Wales, from the local authority in whose area the court which made the order sat; or

(iv) from any other local authority;

(b) if he is in Scotland—

(i) from the regional or islands council in whose area he is living;

      (ii) where the adoption order relating to him was made in Scotland from the council in whose area the court which made the order sat; or

      (iii) from any other regional or islands council;

  (c) if he is in Northern Ireland—

      (i) from the Board in whose area he is living;

      (ii) where the adoption order relating to him was made in Northern Ireland, from the Board in whose area the court which made the order sat; or

      (iii) from any other Board;

  (d) if he is in the United Kingdom and his adoption was arranged by an adoption society—

      (i) approved under section 3,

      (ii) approved under section 3 of the Adoption (Scotland) Act 1978,

      (iii) registered under Article 4 of the Adoption (Northern Ireland) Order 1987,

    from that society.

(4) Where an adopted person who is in England and Wales—

  (a) applies for information under—

      (i) subsection (1), or

      (ii) Article 54 of the Adoption (Northern Ireland) Order 1987, or

  (b) is supplied with information under section 45 of the Adoption (Scotland) Act 1978,

it shall be the duty of the persons and bodies mentioned in subsection (5) to provide counselling for him if asked by him to do so.

(5) The persons and bodies are—

  (a) the Registrar General;

  (b) any local authority falling within subsection (3)(a)(ii) to (iv);

  (c) any adoption society falling within subsection (3)(d) in so far as it is acting as an adoption society in England and Wales.

(6) If the applicant chooses to receive counselling from a person or body falling within subsection (3), the Registrar General shall send to the person or body the information to which the applicant is entitled under subsection (1).

(7) Where a person—

  (a) was adopted before 12th November 1975, and

  (b) applies for information under subsection (1).

the Registrar General shall not supply the information to him unless he has attended an interview with a counsellor arranged by a person or body from whom counselling services are available as mentioned in subsection (3).

(8) Where the Registrar General is prevented by subsection (7) from supplying information to a person who is not living in the United Kingdom, he may supply the information to any body which—

(a) the Registrar General is satisfied is suitable to provide counselling to that person, and

(b) has notified the Registrar General that it is prepared to provide such counselling.

(9) In this section—

"a Board" means a Health and Social Services Board established under Article 16 of the Health and Personal Social Services (Northern Ireland) Order 1972; and
"prescribed" means prescribed by regulations made by the Registrar General.

Adoption Contact Register

51A.—(1) The Registrar General shall maintain at the General Register Office a register to be called the Adoption Contact register.

(2) The register shall be in two parts—

(a) Part I: Adopted Persons; and

(b) Part II: Relatives.

(3) The Registrar General shall, on payment of such fee as may be prescribed, enter in Part I of the register the name and address of any adopted person who fulfils the conditions in subsection (4) and who gives notice that he wishes to contact any relative of his.

(4) The conditions are that—

(a) a record of the adopted person's birth is kept by the Registrar General; and

(b) the adopted person has attained the age of 18 years and—

(i) has been supplied by the Registrar General with information under section 51; or

(ii) has satisfied the Registrar General that he has such information as is necessary to enable him to obtain a certified copy of the record of his birth.

(5) The Registrar General shall, on payment of such fee as may be prescribed, enter in Part II of the register the name and address of any person who fulfils the conditions in subsection (6) and who gives notice that he wishes to contact an adopted person.

(6) The conditions are that—

(a) a record of the adopted person's birth is kept by the Registrar General; and

(b) the person giving notice under subsection (5) has attained the age of 18 years and has satisfied the Registrar General that—

(i) he is a relative of the adopted person; and

(ii) he has such information as is necessary to enable him to obtain a certified copy of the record of the adopted person's birth.

(7) The Registrar General shall, on receiving notice from any person named in an entry in the register that he wishes the entry to be cancelled, cancel the entry.

(8) Any notice given under this section must be in such form as may be determined by the Registrar General.

(9) The Registrar General shall transmit to an adopted person whose name is entered in Part I of the register the name and address of any relative in respect of whom there is an entry in Part II of the register.

(10) Any entry cancelled under subsection (7) ceases from the time of cancellation to be an entry for the purposes of subsection (9).

(11) The register shall not be open to public inspection or search and the Registrar General shall not supply any person with information entered in the register (whether in an uncancelled or a cancelled entry) except in accordance with this section.

(12) The register may be kept by means of a computer.

(13) In this section—

(a) "relative" means any person (other than an adoptive relative) who is related to the adopted person by blood (including half-blood) or marriage;

(b) "address" includes any address at or through which the person concerned may be contacted; and

(c) "prescribed" means prescribed by the Secretary of State.

Revocation of Adoptions on Legitimation

52.—(1) Where any person adopted by his father or mother alone has subsequently become a legitimated person on the marriage of his father and mother, the court by which the adoption order was made may, on the application of any of the parties concerned, revoke that order.

(2) Where any person legitimated by virtue of section 1 of the Legitimacy Act 1959, had been adopted by his father and mother before the commencement of that Act, the court by which the adoption order was made may, on the application of any of the parties concerned, revoke that order.

(3) Where a person adopted by his father or mother alone by virtue of a regulated adoption has subsequently become a legitimated person on the marriage of his father and mother, the High Court may, upon an

application under this subsection by the parties concerned, by order revoke the adoption.

(4) In relation to an adoption order made by a magistrates' court, the reference in subsections (1) and (2) to the court by which the order was made includes a reference to a court acting for the same petty sessions area.

Annulment etc. of Overseas Adoptions

53.—(1) The High Court may, upon an application under this subsection, by order annul a regulated adoption or an adoption effected by a convention adoption order—

(a) on the ground that at the relevant time the adoption was prohibited by a notified provision, if under the internal law then in force in the country of which the adopter was then a national or the adopters were then nationals the adoption could have been impugned on that ground;

(b) on the ground that at the relevant time the adoption contravened provisions relating to consents of the internal law relating to adoption of the country of which the adopted person was then a national, if under that law the adoption could then have been impugned on that ground;

(c) on any other ground on which the adoption can be impugned under the law for the time being in force in the country in which the adoption was effected.

(2) The High Court may, upon an application under this subsection—

(a) order that an overseas adoption or a determination shall cease to be valid in Great Britain on the ground that the adoption or determination is contrary to public policy or that the authority which purported to authorise the adoption or make the determination was not competent to entertain the case;

(b) decide the extent, if any, to which a determination has been affected by a subsequent determination.

(3) Any court in Great Britain may, in any proceedings in that court, decide that an overseas adoption or a determination shall, for the purposes of those proceedings, be treated as invalid in Great Britain on either of the grounds mentioned in subsection (2).

(4) An order or decision of the Court of Session on an application under subsection (3) of section 6 of the Adoption Act 1968 shall be recognised and have effect as if it were an order or decision of the High Court on an application under subsection (3) of this section.

(5) Except as provided by this section and section 52(3) the validity of an overseas adoption or a determination shall not be impugned in England and Wales in proceedings in any court.

Provisions Supplementary to Sections 52(3) and 53

54.—(1) Any application for an order under section 52(3) or 53 or a decision under section 53(3) shall be made in the prescribed manner and within such period, if any, as may be prescribed.

(2) No application shall be made under section 52(3) or section 53(1) in respect of an adoption unless immediately before the application is made the person adopted or the adopter habitually resides in England and Wales or, as the case may be, both adopters habitually reside there.

(3) In deciding in pursuance of section 53 whether such an authority as is mentioned in section 59 was competent to entertain a particular case, a court shall be bound by any finding of fact made by the authority and stated by the authority to be so made for the purpose of determining whether the authority was competent to entertain the case.

(4) In section 53—

"determination" means such a determination as is mentioned in section 59 of this Act;

"notified provision" means a provision specified in an order of the Secretary of State as one in respect of which a notification to or by the Government of the United Kingdom was in force at the relevant time in pursuance of the provisions of the Convention relating to prohibitions contained in the national law of the adopter; and

"relevant time" means the time when the adoption in question purported to take effect under the law of the country in which it purports to have been effected.

Part VI

Miscellaneous and Supplemental

Adoption of Children Abroad

55.—(1) Where on an application made in relation to a child by a person who is not domiciled in England and Wales or Scotland or Northern Ireland an authorised court is satisfied that he intends to adopt the child under the law of or within the country in which the applicant is domiciled, the court may, subject to the following provisions of this section, make an order giving him parental responsibility for the child.

(2) The provisions of Part II relating to adoption orders, except sections 12(1), 14(2), 15(2), 17 to 21 and 25, shall apply in relation to orders under this section as they apply in relation to adoption orders subject to the modification that in section 13(1) for "19" and "13" there are substituted "32" and "26" respectively.

(3) Sections 50 and 51 and paragraphs 1 and 2(1) of Schedule 1 shall apply in relation to an order under this section as they apply in

relation to an adoption order except that any entry in the Registers of Births, or the Adopted Children Register which is required to be marked in consequence of the making of an order under this section shall, in lieu of being marked with the word "Adopted" or "Re-adopted" (with or without the addition of the words "(Scotland)" or "(Northern Ireland)"), be marked with the words "Proposed foreign adoption" or "Proposed foreign re-adoption", as the case may require.

Restriction on Removal of Children for Adoption Outside Great Britain

56.—(1) Except under the authority of an order under section 55, section 49 of the Adoption (Scotland) Act 1978 or Article 57 of the Adoption (Northern Ireland) Order 1987 it shall not be lawful for any person to take or send a child who is a British subject or a citizen of the Republic of Ireland out of Great Britain to any place outside the United Kingdom, the Channel Islands and the Isle of Man with a view to the adoption of the child by any person not being a parent or guardian or relative of the child; and any person who takes or sends a child out of Great Britain to any place in contravention of this subsection, or makes or takes part in any arrangements for placing a child with any person for that purpose, shall be guilty of an offence and liable on summary conviction to imprisonment for a term not exceeding 3 months or to a fine not exceeding level 5 on the standard scale or to both.

(2) In any proceedings under this section, a report by a British consular officer or a deposition made before a British consular officer and authenticated under the signature of that officer shall, upon proof that the officer or the deponent cannot be found in the United Kingdom, be admissible as evidence of the matters stated therein, and it shall not be necessary to prove the signature or official character of the person who appears to have signed any such report or deposition.

(3) A person shall be deemed to take part in arrangements for placing a child with a person for the purpose referred to in subsection (1) if—

    (a) he facilitates the placing of the child with that person; or

    (b) he initiates or takes part in any negotiations of which the purpose or effect is the conclusion of any agreement or the making of any arrangement therefor, and if he causes another person to do so.

Prohibition on Certain Payments

57.—(1) Subject to the provisions of this section, it shall not be lawful to make or give to any person any payment or reward for or in consideration of—

    (a) the adoption by that person of a child;

    (b) the grant by that person of any agreement or consent required in connection with the adoption of a child;

(c) the handing over of a child by that person with a view to the adoption of the child; or

(d) the making by that person of any arrangements for the adoption of a child.

(2) Any person who makes or gives, or agrees or offers to make or give, any payment or reward prohibited by this section, or who receives or agrees to receive or attempts to obtain any such payment or reward, shall be guilty of an offence and liable on summary conviction to imprisonment for a term not exceeding 3 months or to a fine not exceeding level 5 on the standard scale or to both.

(3) This section does not apply to any payment made to an adoption agency by a parent or guardian of a child or by a person who adopts or proposes to adopt a child, being a payment in respect of expenses reasonably incurred by the agency in connection with the adoption of the child, or to any payment or reward authorised by the court to which an application for an adoption order in respect of a child is made.

(3A) This section does not apply to—

(a) any payment made by an adoption agency to a person who has applied or proposes to apply to a court for an adoption order or an order under section 55 (adoption of children abroad), being a payment of or towards any legal or medical expenses incurred or to be incurred by that person in connection with the application; or

(b) any payment made by an adoption agency to another adoption agency in consideration of the placing of a child [with] any person with a view to the child's adoption; or

(c) any payment made by an adoption agency to a voluntary organisation for the time being approved for the purposes of this paragraph by the Secretary of State as a fee for the services of that organisation in putting that adoption agency into contact with another adoption agency with a view to the making of arrangements between the adoption agencies for the adoption of a child.

In paragraph (c) "voluntary organisation" means a body, other than a public or local authority, the activities of which are not carried on for profit.

Permitted Allowances

57A.—(1) The Secretary of State may make regulations for the purpose of enabling adoption agencies to pay allowances to persons who have adopted, or intend to adopt, children in pursuance of arrangements made by the agencies.

(2) Section 57(1) shall not apply to any payment made by an adoption agency in accordance with the regulations.

(3) The regulations may, in particular, make provision as to—

(a) the procedure to be followed by any agency in determining whether a person should be paid an allowance;

(b) the circumstances in which an allowance may be paid;

(c) the factors to be taken into account in determining the amount of an allowance;

(d) the procedure for review, variation and termination of allowances; and

(e) the information about allowances to be supplied by any agency to any person who is intending to adopt a child.

(4) Any scheme approved under section 57(4) shall be revoked as from the coming into force of this section.

(5) Section 57(1) shall not apply in relation to any payment made—

(a) in accordance with a scheme revoked under subsection (4) or section 57(5)(b); and

(b) to a person to whom such payments were made before the revocation of the scheme.

(6) Subsection (5) shall not apply where any person to whom any payments may lawfully be made by virtue of subsection (5) agrees to receive (instead of such payments) payments complying with regulations made under this section.

Restriction on Advertisements

58.—(1) It shall not be lawful for any advertisement to be published indicating—

(a) that the parent or guardian of a child desires to cause a child to be adopted; or

(b) that a person desires to adopt a child; or

(c) that any person (not being an adoption agency) is willing to make arrangements for the adoption of a child.

(2) Any person who causes to be published or knowingly publishes an advertisement in contravention of the provisions of this section shall be guilty of an offence and liable on summary conviction to a fine not exceeding level 5 on the standard scale.

Information Concerning Adoption

58A.—(1) Every local authority and every approved adoption society shall transmit to the Secretary of State, at such times and in such form as he may direct, such particulars as he may require with respect—

(a) to their performance of all or any of their functions under the enactments mentioned in subsection (2) below; and

(b) to the children and other persons in relation to whom they have exercised those functions.

(2) The enactments referred to in subsection (1) above are—

(a) the Adoption Act 1958;

(b) Part I of the Children Act 1975; and

(c) this Act.

(3) The clerk of each magistrates' court shall transmit to the Secretary of State, at such times and in such form as he may direct, such particulars as he may require with respect to the proceedings of the court under the enactments mentioned in subsection (2) above.

(4) The Secretary of State shall publish from time to time abstracts of the particulars transmitted to him under subsections (1) and (3) above.

Effect of Determination and Orders Made in Scotland and Overseas in Adoption Proceedings

59.—(1) Where an authority of a Convention country or any British territory other than the United Kingdom having power under the law of that country or territory—

(a) to authorise or review the authorisation of a regulated adoption or a specified order; or

(b) to give or review a decision revoking or annulling a regulated adoption, a specified order or a Convention adoption order,

makes a determination in the exercise of that power, then, subject to sections 52(3) and 53 and any subsequent determination having effect under this subsection, the determination shall have effect in England and Wales for the purpose of effecting, confirming or terminating the adoption in question or confirming its termination, as the case may be.

(2) Subsections (2) to (4) of section 12 shall apply in relation to an order freeing a child for adoption (other than an order under section 18) as if it were an adoption order; and, on the revocation in Scotland or Northern Ireland of an order freeing a child for adoption, subsections (3) and (3A) of section 20 shall apply as if the order had been revoked under that section.

(3) Sections 12(3) and (4) and 49 apply in relation to a child who is the subject of an order which is similar to an order under section 55 and is made (whether before or after this Act has effect) in Scotland, Northern Ireland, the Isle of Man or any of the Channel Islands, as they apply in relation to a child who is subject of an adoption order.

Evidence of Adoption in Scotland and Northern Ireland

60. Any document which is receivable as evidence of any matter—

(a) in Scotland under section 45 of the Adoption (Scotland) Act 1978; or

(b) in Northern Ireland under Article 63(1) of the Adoption (Northern Ireland) Order 1987,

shall also be so receivable in England and Wales.

Evidence of Agreement and Consent

61.—(1) Any agreement or consent which is required by this Act to be given to the making of an order or application for an order (other than an order to which section 17(6) applies) may be given in writing, and, if the document signifying the agreement or consent is witnessed in accordance with rules, it shall be admissible in evidence without further proof of the signature of the person by whom it was executed.

(2) A document signifying such agreement or consent which purports to be witnessed in accordance with rules shall be presumed to be so witnessed, and to have been executed and witnessed on the date and at the place specified in the document, unless the contrary is proved.

Courts

62.—(1) In this Act, "authorised court", as respects an application for an order relating to a child, shall be construed as follows.

(2) Subject to subsections (4) to (6), if the child is in England or Wales when the application is made, the following are authorised courts—

(a) the High Court;

(b) the county court within whose district the child is, and, in the case of an application for an order freeing a child for adoption, any county court within whose district a parent or guardian of the child is;

(c) any other county court prescribed by rules made under section 102 of the County Courts Act 1959;

(d) a magistrates' court within whose area the child is, and, in the case of an application for an order freeing the child for adoption, a magistrates' court within whose area a parent or guardian of the child is.

(3) If, in the case of an application for an adoption order or for an order freeing a child for adoption, the child is not in Great Britain when the application is made, the High Court is the authorised court.

(4) In the case of an application for a Convention adoption order, paragraphs (b), (c) and (d) of subsection (2) do not apply.

(5) Subsection (2) does not apply in the case of an application under section 29 but for the purposes of such an application the following are authorised courts—

(a) if there is pending in respect of the child an application for an adoption order or an order freeing him for adoption, the court in which that application is pending;

(b) if paragraph (a) does not apply and there is no application for an order under—

(i) section 12 or 18 of the Adoption (Scotland) Act 1978; or

(ii) Article 12, 17 or 18 of the Adoption (Northern Ireland) Order 1987,

the High Court, the county court within whose district the applicant lives and the magistrates' court within whose area the applicant lives.

(6) In the case of an order under section 55, paragraph (d) of subsection (2) does not apply.

(7) Any court to which the proceedings on an application are transferred under any enactment is, as regards the transferred proceedings, an authorised court if it is not an authorised court under the preceding provisions of this section.

Appeals, etc.

63.—

(2) Subject to subsection (3), where on an application to a magistrates' court under this Act the court makes or refuses to make an order, an appeal shall lie to the High Court.

(3) Where an application is made to a magistrates' court under this Act, and the court considers that the matter is one which would more conveniently be dealt with by the High Court, the magistrates' court shall refuse to make an order, and in that case no appeal shall lie to the High Court.

(4) No appeal shall lie to the High Court against an order made under section 34.

Proceedings to be in private

64.—Proceedings under this act—

(a) in the High Court, may be disposed of in chambers;

(b) in a county court, shall be heard and determined in camera.

Guardians ad litem and Reporting Officers

65.—(1) For the purpose of any application for an adoption order or an order freeing a child for adoption or an order under section 20 or 55 rules shall provide for the appointment, in such cases as are prescribed—

(a) of a person to act as guardian ad litem of the child upon the hearing of the application, with the duty of safe-guarding the interests of the child in the prescribed manner;

(b) of a person to act as reporting officer for the purpose of witnessing agreements to adoption and performing such other duties as the rules may prescribe.

(2) A person who is employed—

(a) in the case of an application for an adoption order, by the adoption agency by whom the child was placed; or

(b) in the case of an application for an order freeing a child for adoption, by the adoption agency by whom the application was made; or

(c) in the case of an application under section 20, by the adoption agency with the parental rights and duties relating to the child,

shall not be appointed to act as guardian ad litem or reporting officer for the purposes of the application but, subject to that, the same person may if the court thinks fit be both guardian ad litem and reporting officer.

Panels for Selection of Guardians ad litem and Reporting Officers

65A.—(1) The Secretary of State may by regulations provide for the establishment of panels of persons from whom guardians ad litem and reporting officers appointed under rules made under section 65 must be selected.

(2) The regulations may, in particular, make provision—

(a) as to the constitution, administration and procedure of panels;

(b) requiring two or more specified local authorities to make arrangements for the joint management of a panel;

(c) for the defrayment by local authorities of expenses incurred by members of panels;

(d) for the payment by local authorities of fees and allowances for members of panels;

(e) as to the qualifications for membership of a panel;

(f) as to the training to be given to members of panels;

(g) as to the co-operation required of specified local authorities in the provision of panels in specified areas; and

(h) for monitoring the work of guardians ad litem and reporting officers.

(3) Rules of court may make provision as to the assistance which any guardian ad litem or reporting officer may be required by the court to give to it.

(4) The Secretary of State may, with the consent of the Treasury, make such grants with respect to expenditure of any local authority—

(a) in connection with the establishment and administration of guardian ad litem and reporting officer panels in accordance with section 65;

(b) in paying expenses; fees, allowances and in the provision of training for members of such panels.

as he considers appropriate.

Rules of Procedure

66.—(1) Rules in regard to any matter to be prescribed under this Act and dealing generally with all matters of procedure and incidental matters arising out of this Act and for carrying this Act into effect shall be made by the Lord Chancellor.

(2) Subsection (1) does not apply in relation to proceedings before magistrates' courts, but the power to make rules conferred by section 144 of the Magistrates' Courts Act 1980, shall include power to make provision as to any of the matters mentioned in that subsection.

(3) In the case of—

(a) an application for an adoption order in relation to a child who is not free for adoption;

(b) an application for an order freeing a child for adoption.

rules shall require every person who can be found and whose agreement or consent to the making of the order is required under this Act to be notified of a date and place where he will be heard on the application and of the fact that, unless he wishes or the court requires, he need not attend.

(4) In the case of an application under section 55, rules shall require every parent and guardian of the child who can be found to be notified as aforesaid.

(5) Rules made as respects magistrates' courts may provide for enabling any fact tending to establish the identity of a child with a child to whom a document relates to be proved by affidavit and for excluding or restricting in relation to any facts that may be so proved the power of a justice of the peace to compel the attendance of witnesses.

(6) This section does not apply in relation to sections 9, 10, 11 and 32 to 37.

Orders, Rules and Regulations

67.—(1) Any power to make orders, rules or regulations conferred by this Act on the Secretary of State, the Lord Chancellor or the Registrar General shall be exercisable by statutory instrument.

(2) A statutory instrument containing rules or regulations made under any provision of this Act, except section 3(1), shall be subject to annulment in pursuance of a resolution of either House of Parliament.

(3) An order under section 28(10) or 57(8) shall not be made unless a draft of the order has been approved by resolution of each House of Parliament.

(4) An order made under any provision of this Act, except section 74, may be revoked or varied by a subsequent order under that provision.

(5) Orders and regulations made under this Act may make different provision in relation to different cases or classes of cases and may exclude certain cases or classes of cases.

(6) The Registrar General shall not make regulations under section 51 or paragraph 1(1) of Schedule 1 except with the approval of the Secretary of State.

Offences by Bodies Corporate

68. Where an offence under this Act committed by a body corporate is proved to have been committed with the consent or connivance of or to be attributable to any neglect on the part of, any director, manager, member of the committee, secretary or other officer of the body, he as well as the body shall be deemed to be guilty of that offence and shall be liable to be proceeded against and punished accordingly.

Service of Notices, etc.

69. Any notice or information required to be given under this Act may be given by post.

Nationality

70.—(1) If the Secretary of State by order declares that a description of persons specified in the order has, in pursuance of the Convention, been notified to the Government of the United Kingdom as the description of persons who are deemed to possess the nationality of a particular Convention country, persons of that description shall, subject to the following provisions of this section, be treated for the purposes of this Act as nationals of that country.

(2) Subject to section 54(3) and subsection (3) of this section, where it appears to the court in any proceedings under this Act, or to any court by which a decision in pursuance of section 53(3) falls to be given, that a person is or was at a particular time a national of two or more countries, then—

(a) if it appears to the said court that he is or was then a United Kingdom national, he shall be treated for the purposes of those proceedings or that decision as if he were or had then been a United Kingdom national only;

(b) if, in a case not falling within paragraph (a), it appears to the said court that one only of those countries is or was then a Convention country, he shall be treated for those purposes as if he were or had then been a national of that country only;

(c) if, in a case not falling within paragraph (a), it appears to the said court that two or more of those countries are or were then Convention countries, he shall be treated for those purposes as if he were or had then been a national of such one only of those Convention countries as the said court considers is the country with which he is or was then most closely connected;

(d) in any other case, he shall be treated for those purposes as if he were or had then been a national of such one only of those countries as the said court considers is the country with which he is or was then most closely connected.

(3) A court in which proceedings are brought in pursuance of section 17, 52(3) or 53 shall be entitled to disregard the provisions of subsection (2) in so far as it appears to that court appropriate to do so for the purposes of those proceedings; but nothing in this subsection shall be construed a prejudicing the provisions of section 54(3).

(4) Where, after such inquiries as the court in question considers appropriate, it appears to the court in any proceedings under this Act, or to any court by which such a decision as aforesaid fails to be given, that a person has no nationality or no ascertainable nationality, he shall be treated for the purposes of those proceedings or that decision as a national of the country in which he resides or, where that country is one of two or more countries having the same law of nationality, as a national of those countries.

Internal Law of a Country

71.—(1) In this Act "internal law" in relation to any country means the law applicable in a case where no question arises as to the law in force in any other country.

(2) In any case where the internal law of a country falls to be ascertained for the purposes of this Act by any court and there are in force in that country two or more systems of internal law, the relevant system shall be ascertained in accordance with any rule in force throughout that country indicating which of the systems is relevant in the case in question or, if there is no such rule, shall be the system appearing to that court to be most closely connected with the case.

Interpretation

72.—(1) In this Act, unless the context otherwise requires—

"adoption agency" in sections 11, 13, 18 to 23 and 27 to 31 includes an adoption agency within the meaning of section 1 of the Children Act 1975 (adoption agencies in Scotland);
"adoption order"—

(a) means an order under section 12(1); and

(b) in sections 12(3) and (4), 18 to 20, 27, 28 and 30 to 32 and in the definition of "British adoption order" in this subsection includes an order under section 12 of the Adoption (Scotland) Act 1978 and Article 12 of the Adoption (Northern Ireland) Order 1987 (adoption orders in Scotland and Northern Ireland respectively); and

(c) in sections 27, 28 and 30 to 32 includes an order under section 55, section 49 of the Adoption (Scotland) Act 1978 and Article 57 of the Adoption (Northern Ireland) Order 1987 (orders in relation to children being adopted abroad);

"adoption society" means a body of persons whose functions consist of or include the making of arrangements for the adoption of children;

"approved adoption society" means an adoption society approved under Part I;

"authorised court" shall be construed in accordance with section 62;

"body of persons" means any body of persons, whether incorporated or unincorporated;

"British adoption order" means—

(a) an adoption order as defined in this subsection, and

(c) an order under any provision for the adoption of a child effected under the law of any British territory outside the United Kingdom;

"British territory" means, for the purposes of any provision of this Act, any of the following countries, that is to say, Great Britain, Northern Ireland, the Channel Islands, the Isle of Man and a colony, being a country designated for the purposes of that provision by order of the Secretary of State or, if no country is so designated, any of those countries;

"child", except where used to express a relationship, means a person who has not attained the age of 18 years;

"the Convention" means the Convention relating to the adoption of children concluded at the Hague on 15th November 1965 and signed on behalf of the United Kingdom on that date;

"Convention adoption order" means an adoption order made in accordance with section 17(1);

"Convention country" means any country outside British territory, being a country for the time being designated by an order of the Secretary of State as a country in which, in his opinion, the Convention is in force;

"existing", in relation to an enactment or other instrument, means one passed or made at any time before 1st January 1976;

"guardian" has the same meaning as in the Children Act 1989;

"internal law" has the meaning assigned by section 71;

"local authority" means the council of a county (other than a metropolitan county), a metropolitan district, a London borough or the Common Council of the City of London and, in sections 13, 22, 28 to 31, 35(1) and 51, includes a regional or islands council;

"notice" means a notice in writing;

"order freeing a child for adoption" means an order under section 18 and in sections 27(2) and 59 includes an order under—

(a) section 18 of the Adoption (Scotland) Act 1978; and

(b) Article 17 or 18 of the Adoption (Northern Ireland) Order 1987;

"overseas adoption" has the meaning assigned by subsection (2);

"parent" means, in relation to a child, any parent who has parental responsibility for the child under the Children Act 1989;

"parental responsibility" and "parental responsibility agreement" have the same meaning as in the Children Act 1989;

"place of safety" means a community home provided by a local authority, a controlled community home, police station, or any hospital, surgery or other suitable place the occupier of which is willing temporarily to receive a child;

"prescribed" means prescribed by rules;

"regulated adoption" means an overseas adoption of a description designated by an order under subsection (3) as that of an adoption regulated by the Convention;

"relative" in relation to a child means a grandparent, brother, sister, uncle or aunt, whether of the full blood or half-blood or by affinity and includes, where the child is illegitimate, the father of the child and any person who would be a relative within the meaning of this definition if the child were the legitimate child of his mother and father;

"rules" means rules made under section 66(1) or made by virtue of section 66(2) under section 15 of the Justices of the Peace Act 1949;

"specified order" means any provision for the adoption of a child effected under enactments similar to section 12(1) and 17 in force in Northern Ireland or any British territory outside the United Kingdom;

"United Kingdom national" means, for the purposes of any provision of this Act, a citizen of the United Kingdom and colonies satisfying such conditions, if any, as the Secretary of State may by order specify for the purposes of that provision;

"upbringing" has the same meaning as in the Children Act 1989;

"voluntary organisation" means a body other than a public or local authority the activities of which are not carried on for profit;

(1A) In this Act, in determining with what person, or where, a child has his home, any absence of the child at a hospital or boarding school and any other temporary absence shall be disregarded.

(1B) In this Act, references to a child who is in the care of or looked after by a local authority have the same meaning as in the Children Act 1989.

(2) In this Act "overseas adoption" means an adoption of such a description as the Secretary of State may by order specify, being a description of adoptions of children appearing to him to be effected under the law of any country outside Great Britain; and an order under this subsection may contain provision as to the manner in which evidence of an overseas adoption may be given.

(3) For the purposes of this Act, a person shall be deeded to make arrangements for the adoption of a child if he enters into or makes any agreement or arrangement for, or for facilitating, the adoption of the child by any other person, whether the adoption is effected, or is intended to be effected, in Great Britain or elsewhere, or if he initiates or takes part in any negotiations of which the purpose or effect is the conclusion of any agreement or the making of any arrangement therefor, and if he causes another person to do so.

(4) Except so far as the context otherwise requires, any reference in this Act to an enactment shall be construed as a reference to that enactment as amended by or under any other enactment, including this Act.

(5) In this Act, except where otherwise indicated—

(a) a reference to a numbered Part, section or Schedule is a reference to the Part or section of, or the Schedule to, this Act so numbered, and

(b) a reference in a section to a numbered subsection is a reference to the subsection of that section so numbered, and

(c) a reference in a section, subsection or Schedule to a numbered paragraph is a reference to the paragraph of that section, subsection or Schedule so numbered.

SCHEDULE 1

Registration of Overseas Adoptions

3.—If the Registrar General is satisfied that an entry in the Registers of Births relates to a person adopted under an overseas adoption and that he has sufficient particulars relating to that person to enable an entry, in the form specified for the purposes of this subparagraph in regulations made under paragraph 1(1), to be made in the Adopted Children Register in respect of that person, he shall—

(a) make such an entry in the Adopted Children Register: and

(b) if there is a previous entry in respect of that person in that register, mark the entry (or if there is more than one such entry the last of them) with the word "Re-adopted" followed by the name in brackets of the country in which the adoption was effected; and

(c) unless the entry in the Register of Births is already marked with the word "Adopted" (whether or not followed by other words), mark the entry with that word followed by the name in brackets of the country aforesaid.

Amendment of Orders and Rectification of Registers

4.—(1) The court by which an adoption order has been made may, on the application of the adopter or of the adopted person amend the order by the correction of any error in the particulars contained therein, and may—

(a) if satisfied on the application of the adoptor or the adopted person that within one year beginning with the date of the order any new name has been given to the adopted person (whether in baptism or otherwise), or taken by him, either in lieu of or in addition to a name specified in the particulars required to be entered in the Adopted Children Register in pursuance of the order, amend the order by substituting or adding that name in those particulars, as the case may require;

(b) if satisfied on the application of any person concerned that a diroction for the marking of an entry in the Registers of Births or the Adopted Children Register included in the order in pursuance of sub-paragraph (3) or (4) of paragraph 1 was wrongly so included, revoke that direction.

(2) Where an adoption order is amended or a direction revoked under sub-paragraph (1), the prescribed officer of the court shall cause the amendment to be communicated in the prescribed manner to the Registrar General who shall as the case may require—

(a) cause the entry in the Adopted Children Register to be amended accordingly; or

(b) cause the marking of the entry in the Registers of Births or the Adopted Children Register to be cancelled.

(3) Where an adoption order is quashed or an appeal against an adoption order allowed by any court, the court shall give directions to the Registrar General to cancel any entry in the Adopted Children Register, and any marking of an entry in that Register, or the Registers of Births as the case may be, which was effected in pursuance of the order.

(4) Where an adoption order has been amended, any certified copy of the relevant entry in the Adopted Children Register which may be issued pursuant to subsection (3) of section 50 shall be a copy of the entry as amended, without the reproduction of any note or marking relating to the amendment or of any matter cancelled pursuant thereto; and a copy or extract of an entry in any register, being an entry the marking of which has been cancelled, shall be deemed to be an accurate copy if and only if both the marking and the cancellation are omitted therefrom.

(5) If the Registrar General is satisfied—

(a) that a Convention adoption order or an overseas adoption has ceased to have effect, whether on annulment or otherwise; or

(b) that any entry or mark was erroneously made in pursuance of paragraph 3 in any register mentioned in that paragraph,

he may cause such alterations to be made in any such register as he considers are required in consequence of the cesser or to correct the error; and where an entry in such a register is amended in pursuance of this sub-paragraph, any copy or extract of the entry shall be deemed to be accurate if and only if it shows the entry as amended but without indicating that it has been amended.

(6) In relation to an adoption order made by a magistrates' court, the reference in sub-paragraph (1) to the court by which the order has been made includes a reference to a court acting for the same petty sessions area.

Marking of Entries on Re-registration of Birth on Legitimation

5.—(1) Without prejudice to section 52, where, after an entry in the Register of Births has been marked with the word "Adopted" (with or without the addition of the word "(Scotland)"), the birth is re-registered under section 14 of the Births and Deaths Registration Act 1953 (re-registration of births of legitimated persons) the entry made on the re-registration shall be marked in the like manner.

(2) Without prejudice to paragraph 4(5), where an entry in the Registers of Birth is marked in pursuance of paragraph 3 and the birth in question is subsequently re-registered under the said section 14, the entry made on re-registration shall be marked in the like manner.

Cancellations in Registers on Legitimation

6.—Where an adoption order is revoked under section 52(1) or (2) the prescribed officer of the court shall cause the revocation to be communicated in the prescribed manner to the Registrar General who shall cause to be cancelled—

(a) the entry in the Adopted Children Register relating to the adopted person; and

(b) the marking with the word "Adopted" (or, as the case may be, with that word and the word "(Scotland)") of any entry relating to him in the Registers of Births;

and a copy or extract of an entry in any register, being an entry the marking of which is cancelled under this section, shall be deemed to be an accurate copy if and only if both the marking and the cancellation are omitted therefrom.

NOTE: The Adoption Act is printed as amended.

B. ADOPTION RULES 1984 (S.I. 1984 NO. 265), RR. 27–53

PART IV

Convention Proceedings

Introductory

27.—(1) This Part of these rules shall apply to Convention proceedings and, subject to the provisions of this Part of these rules, Parts I, III and V of these rules shall apply, with the necessary modifications, to Convention proceedings as they apply to proceedings in the High Court under the 1958 Act or Part I of the 1975 Act.

(2) Any reference in this Part of these rules to the nationality of a person who is not solely a United Kingdom national means that person's nationality as determined in accordance with section 9 of the 1968 Act.

Originating Process

28.—(1) An applicant for a Convention adoption order shall state in his originating process that he is applying for a Convention adoption order.

(2) The originating process—

(a) need not contain paragraphs corresponding to paragraphs 2, 24 or 25 of Form 6 but

(b) shall contain the additional information required by Schedule 4 to these rules.

Evidence as to Nationality

29.—(1) Any document (or copy of a document) which is to be used for the purposes of satisfying the court as to the nationality of the applicant or of the child shall be attached to the originating process.

(2) Where the applicant claims that for the purposes of section 24(2)(a), (4)(a), or 5(a) of the 1975 Act he or the child is a national of a Convention country, he shall attach to the originating process a statement by an expert as to the law of that country relating to nationality applicable to that person.

Statement at Hearing

30. The requirement that the conditions in section 24(2), (3) and (4) or (5) of the 1975 Act are satisfied immediately before the order is made may be established by—

(a) oral evidence at the hearing of an application for a Convention adoption order, or

(b) a document executed by the applicant containing a statement to that effect attested in accordance with rule 44 and such a statement shall be admissible in evidence without further proof of the signature of the applicant.

Orders

31. Within 7 days after a Convention adoption order has been drawn up, the proper officer shall by notice to the Registrar General request him to send the information to the designated authorities of any Convention country—

(a) of which the child is a national;

(b) in which the child was born;

(c) in which the applicant habitually resides; or

(d) of which the applicant is a national.

Additional Provisions for Cases where Child is not a United Kingdom National

Scope of Rules 33 to 36

32. Rules 33 to 36 shall apply to any case where the child is not a United Kingdom national, and in such a case—

(a) the provisions in Part III of these rules, other than rules 17 and 20 (agreement to adoption), and

(b) paragraphs 9 to 14 of Form 6,

shall apply with the necessary modifications to take account of section 24(6)*(a)* of the 1975 Act.

Evidence as to Foreign Law Relating to Consents and Consultations

33. The applicant shall file, with his originating process, a statement by an expert as to the provisions relating to consents and consultations of the internal law relating to adoption of the Convention country of which the child is a national.

Form of Consent etc.

34.—(1) Any document signifying the consent of a person to, or otherwise containing the opinion of a person on the making of, the

154

Convention adoption order shall be in a form which complies with the internal law relating to adoption of the Convention country of which the child is a national: provided that where the court is not satisfied that a person consents with full understanding of what is involved, it may call for further evidence.

(2) A document referred to in paragraph (1) shall, if sufficiently witnessed, be admissible as evidence of the consent or opinion contained therein without further proof of the signature of the person by whom it is executed.

(3) A document referred to in paragraph (1) shall, if executed before the date of the applicant's originating process referred to in rule 28(2), be attached to that process.

Notice of Hearing

35.—(1) When serving notice of the hearing on the persons specified in rule 21, the proper officer shall also serve notice on any person:—

(a) whose consent to the making of the order is required, not being an applicant, or

(b) who, in accordance with the internal law relating to adoption of the Convention country of which the child is a national, has to be consulted about, but does not have to consent to, the adoption.

(2) Any person served or required to be served with notice under this rule shall be treated as if he had been served or was required to be served with notice under rule 21.

Proper Officer to Receive Opinions on Adoption

36. For the purposes of this rule and of section 24(7)*(a)* of the 1975 Act, the Senior Registrar of the Principal Registry of the Family Division is the proper officer of the court to whom any person whose consent is required under or who is consulted in pursuance of the internal law relating to adoption of the Convention country of which the child is a national may communicate his consent or other opinion on the adoption.

Proceedings under Section 6 of the 1968 Act

Application to Annul or Revoke Adoption

37.—(1) An application for an order under section 6(1) or (2) of the 1968 Act shall be made by originating process issued out of the Principal Registry of the Family Division in Form 9; and the person filing the process shall be described as the applicant and the adopted person and any adopter, not being the applicant, shall be described as a respondent.

(2) An application under section 6(1) of the 1968 Act shall not, except with the leave of the court, be made later than 2 years after the date of the adoption to which it relates.

Application to Declare Adoption Invalid or Determination Invalid or Affected

38. An application for an order or decision under section 6(3) of the 1968 Act shall be made by originating process out of the Principal Registry of the Family Division in Form 10; and the person filing the process shall be described as the applicant and the adopted person and any adopter, not being the applicant, shall be described as a respondent.

Evidence in Support of Application

39.—(1) Evidence in support of an application under section 6 of the 1968 Act shall be given by means of an affidavit in Form 11 which shall be filed within 14 days after the issue of the originating process.

(2) Where the application is made under section 6(1) or (3) of the 1968 Act there shall be exhibited to the affidavit a statement of the facts and, subject to rule 42, there shall be filed with the affidavit expert evidence of any provision of foreign law relating to adoption on which the applicant intends to rely.

(3) The court may order any deponent to give oral evidence concerning the facts stated in, or exhibited to, his affidavit.

Guardian ad litem

40. Where the adopted person is under the age of 18 on the date on which an application under section 6 of the 1968 Act is made, rule 18(2) and (4) to (7) shall apply to the application as it applies to an application for an adoption order as if the references in rule 18 to the making of an adoption order were references to the granting of an application under section 6 of the 1968 Act.

Notice of Order made under Section 6, etc.

41.—(1) Where under section 6 of the 1968 Act the court has ordered that an adoption be annulled or revoked or that an adoption or a determination shall cease to be valid in Great Britain, the proper officer shall serve notice of the order on the Registrar General, and shall state in the notice—

(a) the date of the adoption;

(b) the name and address of the authority which granted the adoption; and

(c) the names of the adopter or adopters and of the adopted person as given in the affidavit referred to in rule 39.

(2) A notice under paragraph (1) in respect of the annulment or revocation of an adoption shall request the Registrar General to send the information to the designated authorities of any Convention country—

(a) in which the adoption was granted;

(b) of which the adopted person is a national; or

(c) in which the adopted person was born.

(3) Where under section 26(1) of the 1958 Act the court has ordered that a Convention adoption order be revoked, the notice to the Registrar General under section 26(2) of that Act shall request the Registrar General to send the information to the designated authorities of any Convention country—

(a) of which the adopted person is a national; or

(b) in which the adopted person was born.

Supplementary

Evidence as to Specified or Notified Provisions

42.—(1) Where the applicant seeks to satisfy the court as to any question which has arisen or is likely to arise concerning a provision:—

(a) of the internal law of the Convention country of which the applicant or any other person is or was a national,

(b) which has been specified in an order—

(i) under section 24(8) of the 1975 Act (a "specified provision"), or

(ii) under section 7(4) of the 1968 Act (a "notified provision"),

expert evidence of the specified or notified provision shall, where practicable, be attached to the originating process.

(2) Paragraph (1) shall apply, in the case of a person who is or was a United Kingdom national, for the purposes of a notified provision in respect of a specified country as it applies for the purposes of a notified provision in respect of a Convention country of which a person is or was a national.

Interim Order

43. Where the applicant is a national or both applicants are nationals of a Convention country, the court shall take account of any specified provision (as defined in section 24(8) of the 1975 Act) of the internal law of that country before any decision is made to postpone the determination of the application and to make an interim order.

Witnessing of Documents

44. A document shall be sufficiently attested for the purposes of this Part of these rules if it is witnessed by one of the following persons—

(a) if it is executed in England and Wales, the reporting officer, a Justice of the Peace, and officer of a county court appointed for the purposes of section 87 of the County Courts Act 1959(a) or a justices' clerk within the meaning of section 70 of the Justices of the Peace Act 1979(b); or

(b) if it is executed elsewhere, any person specified in rule 8(2), (3) or (4), according to the country in which it is executed.

Service of Documents

45.—(1) Any document to be served for the purposes of this Part of these rules may be served out of the jurisdiction without the leave of the court.

(2) Any document served out of the jurisdiction in a country in which English is not an official language shall be accompanied by a translation of the document in the official language of the country in which service is to be effected or, if there is more than one official language of the country, in any one of those languages which is appropriate to the place in that country where service is to be effected.

Translation of Documents

46. Where a translation of any document is required for the purposes of Convention proceedings, the translation shall, unless otherwise directed, be provided by the applicant.

PART V

Miscellaneous

Application for Removal, Return, etc., of Child

47.—(1) An application—

(a) under section 34(1) or (2) or 34A(1) or (2) of the 1958 Act to remove a child from the actual custody of the person with whom the child has his home, or

(b) under section 30(1) of the 1975 Act for an order for the return of a child who has been removed, in breach of section 34 or 34A of the 1958 Act, from the actual custody of such a person, or

(c) under section 30(2) of the 1975 Act for an order directing a person not to remove a child from the actual custody of such a person, or

(d) under section 35(2) of the 1958 Act for leave to give notice under section 35(1)*(b)* of that Act, or

(e) under section 16(2) of the 1975 Act for leave to place a child for adoption,

shall be made in accordance with paragraph (2).

(2) The application under paragraph (1) shall be made—

(a) if an application for an adoption order or an order under sections 14 or 16 of the 1975 Act is pending, by process on notice in those proceedings; or

(b) if no such application is pending, by filing an originating process in the appropriate court.

(3) The appropriate court for the purposes of paragraph (2)*(b)* shall be the High Court, the county court within whose district the applicant lives or, in the case of an application made under section 34A(2) of the 1958 Act, the court within whose district the child is.

(4) Any respondent to the originating process made under paragraph (2)*(b)* who wishes to claim relief shall do so by means of an answer to the process which shall be made within 7 days of the service of the copy of the process on the respondent.

(5) Subject to paragraph (6), the proper officer shall serve a copy of the process, and of any answer thereto, and a notice of the date of the hearing—

(a) in a case where proceedings for an adoption order or an order under sections 14 or 16 of the 1975 Act are pending (or where such proceedings have subsequently been commenced), on all the parties to those proceedings and on the reporting officer and guardian ad litem, if any;

(b) in any other case, on any person against whom an order is sought in the application and on the local authority to whom the prospective adopter has given notice under section 18 of the 1975 Act; and

(c) in any case, on such other person or body, not being the child, as the court thinks fit.

(6) if in any application under this rule a serial number has been assigned to a person who has applied or who proposes to apply for an adoption order, or such a person applies to the proper officer in that behalf before filing the originating process and a serial number is assigned accordingly—

(a) the proper officer shall ensure that the documents served under paragraph (5) do not disclose the identity of that person to any other party to the application under this rule who is not already aware of that person's identity, and

(b) the proceedings on the application under this rule shall be conducted with a view to securing that he is not seen by or made known to any party who is not already aware of his identity except with his consent.

(7) Unless otherwise directed, any prospective adopter who is served with a copy of an application under this rule and who wishes to oppose the application shall file his process for an adoption order within 14 days or before or at the time of the hearing of the application under this rule, whichever is the sooner.

(8) The court may at any time give directions, and if giving directions under paragraph (7) shall give further directions, as to the conduct of any application under this rule and in particular as to the appointment of a guardian ad litem of the child.

(9) Where an application under paragraph (1)*(a)* or *(d)* is granted or an application under paragraph (1)*(b)* or *(c)* is refused, the judge may thereupon, if process for an adoption order has been filed, treat the hearing of the application as the hearing of the process for an adoption order and refuse an adoption order accordingly.

(10) Where an application under this rule is determined the proper officer shall serve notice of the effect of the determination on all the parties.

(11) Paragraphs (6) to (10) shall apply to an answer made under this rule as they apply to an originating process made under this rule as if the answer were the originating process.

Proposed Foreign Adoption Proceedings

48.—(1) Proceedings for an order authorising a proposed foreign adoption shall be commenced—

(a) by originating summons in Form 6 issued out of the Principal Registry of the Family Division; or

(b) by filing in the office of the county court within whose district the child is an originating application in Form 6.

(2) Subject to paragraph (3), Part III of these rules except rule 15(1) and Part V except rule 52(1)*(d)* shall apply to an application for an order authorising a proposed foreign adoption as if such an order were an adoption order.

(3) An applicant for an order authorising a proposed foreign adoption shall provide expert evidence of the law of adoption in the country in which he is domiciled and an affidavit as to that law sworn by such a person as is mentioned in section 4(1) of the Civil Evidence Act 1972(a) (that is to say a person who is suitably qualified on account of his knowledge or experience to give evidence as to that law) shall be admissible in evidence without notice.

Amendment and Revocation of Orders

49.—(1) An application under section 24 of the 1958 Act for the amendment of an adoption order or the revocation of a direction to the

Registrar General, or under section 26 of the 1958 Act (or section 1(1) of the Adoption Act 1960)(b) for the revocation of an adoption order, may be made ex parte in the first instance, but the court may require notice of the application to be served on such persons as it thinks fit.

(2) Where the application is granted, the proper officer shall send to the Registrar General a notice specifying the amendments or informing him of the revocation and shall give sufficient particulars of the order to enable the Registrar General to identify the case.

Service of Documents

50.—(1) Subject to rule 45 and unless otherwise directed, any document under these rules may be served—

    (a) on a corporation or body of persons, by delivering it at, or sending it by post to, the registered or principal office of the corporation or body;

    (b) on any other person, by delivering it to him, or by sending it by post to him at his usual or last known address.

(2) The person effecting service of any document under these rules shall make, sign, and file a certificate showing the date, place and mode of service. If he has failed to effect service of any document, he shall make, sign and file a certificate of non-service showing the reason why service has not been effected.

Costs

51. On the determination of proceedings to which these rules apply or on the making of an interim order, the judge may make such order as to the costs as he thinks just and, in particular, may order the applicant to pay—

    (a) the expenses incurred by the reporting officer and the guardian ad litem (if appointed),

    (b) the expenses incurred by any respondent in attending the hearing,

or such part of those expenses as the judge thinks proper.

Notice and Copies of Orders, etc.

52.—(1) In proceedings to which these rules apply orders shall be made in the form indicated in this paragraph—

Description of order	*Form*
(a) Order under section 14 of the 1975 Act	12
(b) Order under section 16 of the 1975 Act	13
(c) Interim order	14
(d) Adoption order	15
(e) Convention adoption order	15 (with the word "Convention" inserted where appropriate)
(f) Order authorising a proposed foreign adoption	15 (with the words "order authorising a proposed foreign adoption" substituted for the words "adoption order" wherever they appear).

(2) Where an adoption order is made by a court sitting in Wales in respect of a child who was born in Wales (or is treated under rule 24(4) as having been born in the registration district and sub-district in which that court sits) and the adopter so requests before the order is drawn up, the proper officer shall obtain a translation into Welsh of the particulars set out in the order.

(3) Within 7 days of the making of an order in proceedings to which these rules apply, the proper officer shall send a copy of the order (and of any translation into Welsh obtained under paragraph (2)) to the applicant.

(4) Within 7 days of the making of an order to which paragraph (1)*(d)*, *(e)* or *(f)* applies, the proper officer shall send a copy of the order (and of any translation into Welsh obtained under paragraph (2)) to the Registrar General and, in the case of a Convention adoption order, shall comply with rule 31; where a translation into Welsh under paragraph (2) has been obtained, the English text shall prevail.

(5) Where an order to which paragraph (1)*(a)*, *(b)*, *(d)*, *(e)* or *(f)* applies is made or refused or an order to which paragraph (1)*(c)* applies is made, the proper officer shall serve notice to that effect on every respondent.

(6) Where, on the refusal of an adoption order, any order under section 17 of the 1975 Act (care etc. of child on refusal of adoption order) is made, the notice under paragraph (5) shall include particulars of that order.

(7) The proper officer shall serve notice of the making of an order to which paragraph (1)*(a)*, *(b)*, *(d)*, *(e) or (f)* applies on any court in Great Britain which appears to him to have made any such order as is referred to in section 8(3) of the 1975 Act (orders relating to the parental rights and duties and the maintenance of the child).

(8) A copy of any order may be supplied to the Registrar General at his request.

(9) A copy of any order may be supplied to the applicant.

(10) A copy of any order may be supplied to any other person with the leave of the court.

Custody, Inspection and Disclosure of Documents and Information

53.—(1) All documents relating to proceedings under the 1958 Act, the 1968 Act or Part I or the 1975 Act (or under any previous enactment relating to adoption) shall, while they are in the custody of the court, be kept in a place of special security.

(2) A party who is an individual and is referred to in a confidential report supplied to the court by an adoption agency, a local authority, a reporting officer or a guardian ad litem may inspect, for the purposes of the hearing, that part of any such report which refers to him, subject to any direction given by the court that—

   (a) no part of one or any of the reports shall be revealed to that party, or

   (b) the part of one or any of the reports referring to that party shall be revealed only to that party's legal advisers, or

   (c) the whole or any other part of one or any of the reports shall be revealed to that party.

(3) Any person who obtains any information in the course of, or relating to, any proceedings mentioned in paragraph (1) shall treat that information as confidential and shall only disclose it if—

   (a) the disclosure is necessary for the proper exercise of his duties, or

   (b) the information is requested—
      (i) by a court or public authority (whether in Great Britain or not) having power to determine adoptions and related matters, for the purpose of the discharge of its duties in that behalf, or
      (ii) by the Registrar General, or a person authorised in writing by him, where the information requested relates only to the identity of any adoption agency which made the arrangements for placing the child for adoption in the actual custody of the applicants, and of any local authority which was notified of the applicant's intention to apply for an adoption order in respect of the child, or
      (iii) by a person who is authorised in writing by the Secretary of State to obtain the information for the purposes of research.

(4) Save as required or authorised by a provision of any enactment or of these rules or with the leave of the court, no document or order held by or lodged with the court in proceedings under the 1958 Act, the 1968 Act or Part I of the 1975 Act (or under any previous enactment relating to adoption) shall be open to inspection by any person, and no copy of any such document or order, or of an extract from any such document or order, shall be taken by or issued to any person.

C. CHILDREN ACT 1989, SCHED. 2, PARA. 19

SCHEDULE 2

Arrangements to Assist Children to Live Abroad

19.—(1) A local authority may only arrange for, or assist in arranging for, any child in their care to live outside England and Wales with the approval of the court.

(2) A local authority may, with the approval of every person who has parental responsibility for the child arrange for, or assist in arranging for, any other child looked after by them to live outside England and Wales.

(3) The court shall not give its approval under sub-paragraph (1) unless it is satisfied that—

(a) living outside England and Wales would be in the child's best interests;

(b) suitable arrangements have been, or will be, made for his reception and welfare in the country in which he will live;

(c) the child has consented to living in that country; and

(d) every person who has parental responsibility for the child has consented to his living in that country.

(4) Where the court is satisfied that the child does not have sufficient understanding to give or withhold his consent, it may disregard sub-paragraph (3)(c) and give its approval if the child is to live in the country concerned with a parent, guardian, or other suitable person.

(5) Where a person whose consent is required by sub-paragraph (3)(d) fails to give his consent, the court may disregard that provision and give its approval if it is satisfied that that person—

(a) cannot be found;

(b) is incapable of consenting; or

(c) is withholding his consent unreasonably.

(6) Section 56 of the Adoption Act 1976 (which requires authority for the taking or sending abroad for adoption of a child who is a British subject) shall not apply in the case of any child who is to live outside

England and Wales with the approval of the court given under this paragraph.

(7) Where a court decides to give its approval under this paragraph it may order that its decision is not to have effect during the appeal period.

(8) In sub-paragraph (7) "the appeal period" means—

    (a) where an appeal is made against the decision, the period between the making of the decision and the determination of the appeal; and

    (b) otherwise, the period during which an appeal may be made against the decision.

D. IMMIGRATION RULES 1980, RR. 53-55

CHILDREN

53. If the requirements of paragraph 52 are satisfied, children under 18, provided that they are unmarried, are to be admitted for settlement:

(a) if both parents are settled in the United Kingdom; or

(b) if both parents are on the same occasion admitted for settlement; or

(c) if one parent is settled in the United Kingdom and the other is on the same occasion admitted for settlement; or

(d) if one parent is dead and other parent is settled in the United Kingdom or is on the same occasion admitted for settlement; or

(e) if one parent is settled in the United Kingdom or is on the same occasion admitted for settlement and has had the sole responsibility for the child's upbringing; or

(f) if one parent or a relative other than a parent is settled or accepted for settlement in the United Kingdom and there are serious and compelling family or other considerations which make exclusion undesirable — for example, where the other parent is physically or mentally incapable of looking after the child — and suitable arrangements have been made for the child's care.

In this paragraph 'parent' includes the stepfather of a child whose father is dead; the stepmother of a child whose mother is dead; and the father as well as the mother of an illegitimate child. It also includes an adoptive parent, but only where there has been a genuine transfer or parental responsibility on the ground of the original parents' inability to care for the child, and the adoption is not one of convenience arranged to facilitate the child's admission.

54. If the requirements of paragraph 52 are satisfied, children under 18, provided that they are unmarried, are to be admitted for an initial period of up to 12 months:

(a) if one parent is to settle in the United Kingdom or is on the same occasion admitted for settlement and the other is given limited leave with a view to settlement; or

(b) if they meet the requirements of sub-paragraphs (e) or (f) of paragraph 53 but for the fact that they are joining or accompanying one parent given limited leave with a view to settlement.

In this paragraph 'parent' is as defined paragraph 53.

167

55. Children aged 18 or over must qualify for settlement in their own right unless there are the most exceptional compassionate circumstances (in which case their cases should be considered under paragraph 56). Special consideration may, however, be given to fully dependent and unmarried daughters over 18 and under 21 who formed part of the family unit overseas and have no other close relatives in their own country to turn to. The requirements of paragraph 52 must be met in all cases.

E. STATEMENT OF CHANGES IN THE IMMIGRATION RULES 1994 (H.C. 395), PARAS. 310-316

ADOPTED CHILDREN

Requirements for Indefinite Leave to enter the United Kingdom as the Adopted Child of a Parent or Parents Present and Settled or Being Admitted for Settlement in the United Kingdom

310.—The requirements to be met in the case of a child seeking indefinite leave to enter the United Kingdom as the adopted child of a parent or parents present and settled or being admitted for settlement in the United Kingdom are that he:

(i) is seeking leave to enter to accompany or join an adoptive parent or parents in one of the following circumstances;

    (a) both parents are present and settled in the United Kingdom; or

    (b) both parents are being admitted on the same occasion for settlement; or

    (c) one parent is present and settled in the United Kingdom and the other is being admitted on the same occasion for settlement; or

    (d) one parent is present and settled in the United Kingdom or being admitted on the same occasion for settlement and the other parent is dead; or

    (e) one parent is present and settled in the United Kingdom or being admitted on the same occasion for settlement and has had sole responsibility for the child's upbringing; or

    (f) one parent is present and settled in the United Kingdom or being admitted on the same occasion for settlement and there are serious and compelling family or other considerations which make exclusion of the child undesirable and suitable arrangements have been made for the child's care; and

(ii) is under the age of 18; and

(iii) is not leading an independent life, is unmarried, and has not formed an independent family unit; and

(iv) can, and will, be maintained and accommodated adequately without recourse to public funds in accommodation which the adoptive parent or parents own or occupy exclusively; and

(v) was adopted in accordance with a decision taken by the competent administrative authority or court in his country of origin or the country in which he is resident; and

(vi) was adopted at a time when:

(a) both adoptive parents were resident together abroad; or

(b) either or both adoptive parents were settled in the United Kingdom; and

(vii) has the same rights and obligaitons as any other child of the marriage; and

(viii) was adopted due to the inability of the original parent(s) or current carer(s) to care for him and there has been a genuine transfer of parental responsibility to the adoptive parents; and

(ix) has lost or broken his ties with his family of origin; and

(x) was adopted, but the adoption is not one of convenience arranged to facilitate his admission to or remaining in the United Kingdom; and

(xi) holds a valid United Kingdom entry clearance for entry in this capacity.

Requirements for Indefinite Leave to Remain in the United Kingdom as the Adopted Child of a Parent or Parents Present and Settled in the United Kingdom

311.—The requirements to be met in the case of a child seeking indefinite leave to remain in the United Kingdom as the adopted child of a parent or parents present and settled in the United Kingdom are that he:

is seeking to remain with an adoptive parent or parents in one of the following circumstances:

(a) both parents are present and settled in the United Kingdom; or

(b) one parent is present and settled in the United Kingdom and the other parent is dead; or

(c) one parent is present and settled in the United Kingdom and has had sole responsibility for the child's upbringing; or

(d) one parent is present and settled in the United Kingdom and there are serious and compelling family or other considerations which make exclusion of the child undesirable and suitable arrangements have been made for the child's care; and

(ii) has limited leave to enter or remain in the United Kingdom, and

(a) is under the age of 18; or

(b) was given leave to enter or remain with a view to settlement under paragraph 315; and

(iii) is not leading an independent life, is unmarried, and has not formed an independent family unit; and

(iv) can, and will, be maintained and accommodated inadequately without recourse to public funds in accommodation which the adoptive parent or parents own or occupy exclusively; and

(v) was adopted in accordance with a decision taken by the competent administrative authority or court in his country of origin or the country in which he is resident; and

(vi) was adopted at a time when:
(a) both adoptive parents were resident together abroad; or
(b) either or both adoptive parents were settled in the United Kingdom; and

(vii) has the same rights and obligations as any other child of the marriage; and

(viii) was adopted due to the inability of the original parent(s) or current carer(s) to care for him and there has been a genuine transfer of parental responsibility to the adoptive parents; and

(ix) has lost or broken his ties with his family of origin; and

(x) was adopted, but the adoption is not one of convenience arranged to facilitate his admission to or remaining in the United Kingdom.

Indefinite Leave to Enter or Remain in the United Kingdom as the Adopted Child of a Parent or Parents Present and Settled or Being Admitted for Settlement in the United Kingdom

312.—Indefinite leave to enter the United Kingdom as the adopted child of a parent or parents present and settled or being admitted for settlement in the United Kingdom may be granted provided a valid United Kingdom entry clearance for entry in this capacity is produced to the Immigration Officer on arrival. Indefinite leave to remain in the United Kingdom as the adopted child of a parent or parents present and settled in the United Kingdom may be granted provided the Secretary of State is satisfied that each of the requirements of paragraph 311 is met.

Refusal of Indefinite Leave to Enter or Remain in the United Kingdom as the Adopted Child of a Parent or Parents Present and Settled or Being Admitted for Settlement in the United Kingdom

313.—Indefinite leave to enter the United Kingdom as the adopted child of a parent or parents present and settled or being admitted for settlement in the United Kingdom is to be refused if a valid United Kingdom entry clearance for entry in this capacity is not produced to the Immigration Officer on arrival. Indefinite leave to remain in the United Kingdom as the adopted child of a parent or parents present and settled in the United Kingdom is to be refused if the Secretary of State is not satisfied that each of the requirements of paragraph 311 is met.

Requirements for Limited Leave to Enter or Remain in the United Kingdom with a View to Settlement as the Adopted Child of a Parent or Parents Given Limited Leave to Enter or Remain in the United Kingdom with a View to Settlement

314.—The requirements to be met in the case of a child seeking limited leave to enter or remain in the United Kingdom with a view to settlement as the adopted child of a parent or parents given limited leave to enter or remain in the United Kingdom with a view to settlement are that he:

(i) is seeking leave to enter to accompany or join or remain with a parent or parents in one of the following circumstances:

(a) one parent is present and settled in the United Kingdom or being admitted on the same occasion for settlement and the other parent is being or has been given limited leave to enter or remain in the United Kingdom with a view to settlement; or

(b) one parent is being or has been given limited leave to enter or remain in the United Kingdom with a view to settlement and has had sole responsibility for the child's upbringing; or

(c) one parent is being or has been given limited leave to enter or remain in the United Kingdom with a view to settlement and there are serious and compelling family or other considerations which make exclusion of the child undesirable and suitable arrangements have been made for the child's care, and

(ii) is under the age of 18; and

(iii) is not leading an independent life, is unmarried, and has not formed an independent family unit; and

(iv) can, and will, be maintained and accommodated adequately without recourse to public funds in accommodation which the adoptive parent or parents own or occupy exclusively; and

(v) was adopted in accordance with a decision taken by the competent administrative authority or court in his country of origin or the country in which he is resident; and

(vi) was adopted at a time when:

(a) both adoptive parents were resident together abroad; or

(b) either or both adoptive parents were settled in the United Kingdom; and

(vii) has the same rights and obligations as any other child of the marriage; and

(viii) was adopted due to the inability of the original parent(s) or current carer(s) to care for him and there has been a genuine transfer of parental responsibility to the adoptive parents; and

(ix) has lost or broken his ties with his family of origin; and

(x) was adopted, but the adoption is not one of convenience arranged to facilitate his admission to the United Kingdom; and

(xi) (where an application is made for limited leave to remain with a view to settlement) has limited leave to enter or remain in the United Kingdom; and

(xii) if seeking leave to enter, holds a valid United Kingdom entry clearance for entry in this capacity.

Limited Leave to Enter or Remain in the United Kingdom with a View to Settlement as the Adopted Child of a Parent or Parents given Limited Leave to Enter or Remain in the United Kingdom with a View to Settlement

315.—A person seeking limited leave to enter the United Kingdom with a view to settlement as the adopted child of a parent or parents given limited leave to enter or remain in the United Kingdom with a view to settlement may be admitted for a period not exceeding 12 months provided he is able, on arrival, to produce to the Immigration Officer a valid United Kingdom entry clearance for entry in this capacity. A person seeking limited leave to remain in the United Kingdom with a view to settlement as the adopted child of a parent or parents given limited leave to enter or remain in the United Kingdom with a view to settlement may be granted limited leave for a period not exceeding 12 months provided the Secretary of State is satisfied that each of the requirements of paragraph 314 (i)–(xi) is met.

Refusal of Limited Leave to Enter or Remain in the United Kingdom With a View to Settlement as the Adopted Child of a Parent or Parents Given Limited Leave to Enter or Remain in the United Kingdom with a View to Settlement

316.—Limited leave to enter the United Kingdom with a view to settlement as the adopted child of a parent or parents given limited leave to enter or remain in the United Kingdom with a view to settlement is to be refused if a valid United Kingdom entry clearance for entry in this capacity is not produced to the Immigration Officer on arrival. Limited leave to remain in the United Kingdom with a view to settlement as the adopted child of a parent or parents given limited leave to enter or remain in the United Kingdom with a view to settlement is to be refused if the Secretary of State is not satisfied that each of the requirements of paragraph 314 (i)–(xi) is met.

F. FAMILY PROCEEDINGS RULES 1991 (S.I. 1991 NO. 1247), R. 3.15

Application Under Section 57 the of Act of 1986 for Declaration as to Adoption Effected Overseas

315.—(1) Unless otherwise directed, a petition by which proceedings are begun under section 57 of the Act of 1986 for a declaration as to an adoption effected overseas shall state —

(a) the names of those persons who are to be respondents pursuant to paragraph (4) and the residential address of each of them at the date of the presentation of the petition;

(b) the date and place of the petitioner's birth;

(c) the date and place of the adoption order and the court or other tribunal or authority which made it;

(d) all other material facts alleged by the petitioner to justify the making of the declaration and the grounds on which the application is made;

(e) either that the petitioner is domiciled in England and Wales on the date of the presentation of the petition or that he has been habitually resident in England and Wales throughout the period of one year ending with that date.

(2) There shall be annexed to the petition a copy of the petitioner's birth certificate (if it is available this certificate should be the one made after the adoption referred to in the petition) and, unless otherwise directed, a certified copy of the adoption order effected under the law of any country outside the British Islands.

(3) Where a document produced by virtue of paragraph (2) is not in English, it shall, unless otherwise directed, be accompanied by a translation certified by a notary public or authenticated by affidavit.

(4) The following shall, if alive, be respondents to the application, either—

(a) those whom the petitioner claims are his adoptive parents for the purposes of section 39 of the Adoption Act 1976; or

(b) those whom the petitioner claims are not his adoptive parents for the purposes of that section.

G. ADOPTION (DESIGNATION OF OVERSEAS ADOPTIONS) ORDER 1973 (S.I. 1973 NO. 19)

Schedule

Part I

Commonwealth Countries and United Kingdom Dependent Territories

Australia
Bahamas
Barbados
Bermuda
Botswana
British Honduras *[now Belize]*
British Virgin Islands
Canada
Cayman Islands
The Republic of Cyprus
Dominica
Fiji
Ghana
Gibraltar
Guyana
Hong Kong
Jamaica
Kenya
Lesotho
Malawi
Malaysia

Malta
Mauritius
Montserrat
New Zealand
Nigeria
Pitcairn
St Christopher, Nevis and Anguilla
St Vincent
Seychelles
Singapore
Southern Rhodesia *[now Zimbabwe]*
Sri Lanka
Swaziland
Tanzania
Tonga
Trinidad and Tobago
Uganda
Zambia

Part II

Other Countries and Territories

Austria
Belgium
Denmark (including Greenland and the Faroes)
Finland

France (including Réunion, Martinique, Guadeloupe and French Guyana)
The Federal Republic of Germany and Land Berlin (West Berlin)
Greece
Iceland
The Republic of Ireland
Israel
Italy
Luxembourg
The Netherlands (including Surinam and the Antilles)
Norway
Portugal (including the Azores and Madeira)
South Africa and South West Africa *[now Namibia]*
Spain (including the Balearics and the Canary Islands)
Sweden
Switzerland
Turkey
The United States of America
Yugoslavia

Appendix 3

PRECEDENTS

A. ORIGINATING PROCESS FOR AN ADOPTION ORDER/ORDER AUTHORISING A PROPOSED FOREIGN ADOPTION

Form 6

(Heading as in Form 1)

I/We, the undersigned,   (and   ,) wishing to adopt   , a child, hereby give the following further particulars in support of my/our application.

Part I

Particulars of the applicant(s)

  1. *Name and address etc.*

Name of (first) applicant in full

Address

Occupation

Date of Birth

Relationship (if any) to the child

(Name of (second) applicant in full

Address

Occupation

Date of Birth

Relationship (if any) to the child

  2. *Domicile*

I am/we are/one of us (namely   ) is domiciled in England and Wales/Scotland/Northern Ireland/the Channel Islands/the Isle of Man.

  3. *Status*

We are married to each other and our marriage certificate (or other evidence of marriage) is attached (*or* I am unmarried/a widow/a widower/a divorcee) (*or* I am applying alone as a married person and can satisfy the court that   ).

4. I am applying alone for an adoption order in respect of my own child and can satisfy the court that the other natural parent
.)

5. *Health*

A report on my/our health, made by a registered medical practitioner on the   day of 19   , is attached.)

Part 2

Particulars of the child.

6. *Identity etc.*

The child is of the   sex and is not and has not been married. He/she was born on the   day of
19   and is the person to whom the attached birth/adoption certifi-cate relates (*or* was born on or about the   day of
19   , in   ). He/she is a
national.

(7. *Health*

A report on the health of the child, made by a registered medical practitioner on the   day of   19   , is attachcd.)

(8. The child is free for adoption pursuant to section 14 of the Children Act 1975, and I/we attach hereto the order of the   court, dated   , to that effect. The parental rights and duties relating to the child were thereby vested in   (and were transferred to   by order of the   court under section 23 of the Children Act 1975 on
19   ).)

(9. *Parentage, etc.*

The child is the child of   whose last known address was
(*or* deceased) and   whose last known address was
(*or* deceased).)

(10. The guardian(s) of the child (other than the mother or the father of the child) is/are   of   (and
of   ).)

(11. *Parental agreement*

I/We understand that the said
(and   ) is/are willing to agree to the making of an adoption order in pursuance of my/our application.)

(12. I/we request the judge to dispense with the agreement of
(and   ) on the ground(s) that
(and   ) and there are attached hereto three copies of a statement of the facts upon which I/we intend to rely.)

(13. *Care etc.*
The child is in the care of   (who have the powers and
duties of a parent or guardian of the child) (*or* the parental rights and
duties in respect of the child).)

(14. *Maintenance*
                              of   is liable by virtue of an
order made by the   court at   on
the   day of   19   , (*or* by an agreement dated the   day of   19   ) to contrib-
ute to the maintenance of the child.)

15. *Proposed names*
If an adoption order is made in pursuance of this application, the child
is to be known by the following names:
Surname
Other names

Part 3

General

16. The child has lived with me/us continuously since the date of
        19   (and has accordingly had his home with me/us for the
five years preceding the date of this application).

17. The child was (placed with me/us for adoption on the
day of   19   , by   , an adoption agency) (*or*
received into my/our actual custody in the following circumstances:
).

(18. I/we notified the   Council on the
day of   19   , of my/our intention to apply for an
adoption order in respect of the child.)

19. No proceedings relating in whole or in part to the child other than
as stated in paragraph 8 have been completed or commenced in any
court in England and Wales or elsewhere (except   .)

20. I/we have not received or given any payment or reward for, or in
consideration of, the adoption of the child, for any agreement to the
making of an adoption order, the transfer of the actual custody of the
child with a view to adoption or the making of any arrangements for
adoption (except as follows:—   ).

21. As far as I/we know, the only person(s) or body(y)(ies) who have taken part in the arrangements for the child's adoption are

(22. For the purpose of this application reference may be made to   of   .)

(23. I/we desire that my/our identity should be kept confidential, and the serial number of this application is   .)

(24. I/we intend to adopt the child under the law of or within   which is the country of my/our domicile, and evidence as to the law of adoption in that country is filed with this process.)

(25. I/we desire to remove the child from the British Isles for the purpose of adoption.)
I/we accordingly apply for an adoption order/an order authorising a proposed foreign adoption in respect of the child.
Dated this   day of   19   .

Signature(s)

B. MODIFICATION TO FORM 6 FOR THE PURPOSES OF CONVENTION PROCEEDINGS

Form 6 shall contain the following additional paragraphs after paragraph 25:

"Part IV
Additional Information Required for a Convention Adoption Application
26. *The Child.*
The child—

(a) is a United Kingdom national (*or* a national of   which is a Convention country) and

(b) habitually resides at   which is in British territory (*or* a Convention country).

27. *The Applicants*
We are applying together, in reliance on section 24(4)(a) of the 1975 Act, and the first applicant is a United Kingdom national (*or* a national of   which is a Convention country) and the second applicant is a United Kingdom national (*or* a national of which is a Convention country) and we habitually reside at   which is in Great Britain.
(*or*
27. *The Applicants*
We are applying together in reliance on section 24(4)(b) of the 1975 Act, and are both United Kingdom nationals, and we are habitually resident at   which is in British territory (*or* a Convention country).)
(*or*
27. *The Applicant*
I am applying alone in reliance on section 24(5)(a) of the 1975 Act, and am a United Kingdom national (*or* a national of   which is a Convention country) and habitually reside at   which is in Great Britain.)
(*or*
27. *The Applicant*
I am applying alone in reliance on section 24(5)(b) of the 1975 Act, and am a United Kingdom national and habitually reside at   which is in British territory (*or* a Convention country).)
28. *Specified Provisions*
We are both (*or* I am), accordingly, nationals of the same (*or* a national of a) Convention country, namely   and there are no specified provisions in respect of that country (*or* there are no relevant specified provisions in respect of that country because   ).)

C. PETITION FOR RECOGNITION OF AN ADOPTION EFFECTED INSIDE THE BRITISH ISLANDS BY THE LAW OF ENGLAND AND WALES IN THE HIGH COURT OF JUSTICE FAMILY DIVISION

Between
and

Petitioner
Respondent

The petition shows that:

1. The petitioner was born on   day of 19   at   . His parents died on   /abandoned him on   . The petitioner then went to live with at   who formally undertook to be responsible for the upbringing of the petitioner coupled with a declaration of adoption under notarial seal on the   day of   19   at   . The respondent is and was at the date of the declaration of adoption domiciled at   by the said domestic law the declaration made the petitioner the lawful child of the respondent.

2. The petitioner has been habitually resident in England and Wales at the address at   throughout the period of one year ending with the date of presentation of this petition.

3. The grounds upon which this application for a declaration are made are   wherefore the petitioner prays that it may be declared that the validity of the adoption effected by means of the said declaration dated the   day of   19   be recognised in England and Wales for all purposes and that the petitioner is for the purposes of section 39 of the Adoption Act 1976 the adopted child of the respondent.

Signed
Solicitor for Petitioner

The address of the Respondent is

D. NOTICE OF HEARING OF AN APPLICATION FOR AN ADOPTION ORDER/ AN ORDER AUTHORISING A PROPOSED FOREIGN ADOPTION

Form 8

(Heading as in Form I)

To   of
Whereas an application for an adoption order/an order authorising a proposed foreign adoption in respect of   , a child of the   sex born on the   day of   19
    , has been made (by   (and   ) of
) (*or* under the serial number   ) and whereas
                  (and   ) was/were appointed reporting officer(s) (and   was appointed guardian ad litem of the child);

TAKE NOTICE:—

(1. That the said application will be heard before the judge at   on the   day of   19   , at   o'clock and that you may then appear and be heard on the question whether an adoption order/an order authorising a proposed foreign adoption should be made.)

(2. That if you wish to appear and be heard on the question whether an adoption order/an order authorising a proposed foreign adoption should be made, you should give notice to the court on or before the   day of   19   , in order that a time may be fixed for your appearance.)

(3. That you are not obliged to attend the hearing unless you wish to do so or the court notifies you that your attendance is necessary.

(4. That while the application is pending, a parent or guardian of the child who has agreed to the making of an order must not, except with the leave of the court, remove the child from the actual custody of the applicant.

(5. That the application states that the child has had his home with the applicant for the five years preceding the application and accordingly, if that is correct, no person is entitled, against the will of the applicant, to remove the child from the applicant's actual custody except with the leave of the court or under authority conferred by an enactment or on the arrest of the child.)

(6. That the court has been requested to dispense with your agreement to the making of an order on the ground(s) that   and a statement of the facts on which the applicant intends to rely is attached.)

Form 8

It would assist the court if you would complete the attached form and return it to me.

Dated the   day of   19   .

Registrar

To the Senior Registrar of the Principal Registry of the Family Division/
Registrar of the   county court.

No.

I received the notice of the hearing of the application on the
          day of   19   .

I wish/do not wish to oppose the application.

I wish/do not wish to appear and be heard on the question whether an order should be made.

(signature)

(address)

(date)

E. DECLARATION AS TO AN ADOPTION EFFECTED OVERSEAS UNDER SECTION 57 OF THE FAMILY LAW ACT 1986

Form M32

(Heading as in matter)

Upon the petition of   *(the petitioner)* and upon hearing   *(the petitioner)* and upon hearing   *(the respondent)*:

It is declared* that, because the said   , the petitioner was [*or* was not] adopted for the purposes of section 72(2) of the Adoption Act 1976 on the   day of   19   , in   *(country where the adoption took place or did not take place)* in   *(the actual or alleged adoptive parent)*, then for the purposes of section 39 of the Adoption Act 1976 the said   , the petitioner, is [*or* is not] the adopted child of the said   *(the actual or alleged adoptive parent)*.

Dated

F. (CONVENTION) ADOPTION ORDER/ ORDER AUTHORISING A PROPOSED FOREIGN ADOPTION

Form 15

(Heading as in Form 1)

Whereas an application has been made by   of whose   occupation   is
(and   whose   occupation   is
) for an adoption order/an order authorising a proposed foreign adoption/a Convention adoption order in respect of
, a child of the   sex, the child/ adopted child of   (and   );

It is ordered that (the applicant(s) do adopt the child) *(or* the applicant(s) be authorised to remove the child from Great Britain for the purpose of adopting him/her under the law of or within the country in which the applicant is/applicants are domiciled, and that the parental rights and duties relating to the child (including the legal custody of the child) be vested in the applicant(s).

(And as regards costs, it is ordered that   ;)

(And it is recorded that the   , being an adoption agency, placed the child for adoption with the applicant(s)/the
Council was notified of the applicant(s) intention to adopt the child;)

(And   whereas   the   child   was   freed   for   adoption   by   the
court   on   the   day   of
19   ;)

(And whereas the precise date of the child's birth has not been proved to the satisfaction of the court but the court has determined the probable date of his/her birth to be the   day of
19   ;)

(And whereas it has been proved to the satisfaction of the court that the child was born in   (country);)

(And whereas the place of birth of the child has not been proved to the satisfaction of the court (but it appears probable that the child was born in the United Kingdom, the Channel Islands or the Isle of Man, the

child is treated as having been born in the registration district of
and sub-district of   in the county of
);)

(And whereas it has been proved to the satisfaction of the court that
the child was born on the   day of
19   (and is identical with   to whom the entry numbered
made on the   day of   19   ,
in the Register of Births for the registration district of   and
sub-district of   in the county of   relates) (or
with   to whom the entry numbered   and
dated the   day of   19   , in the Adopted
Children Register relates);)

(And whereas the name or names and surname stated in the
application as those by which the child is to be known are
;)

It is directed that the Registrar General shall make in the Adopted
Children Register an entry in the form specified by regulations made by
him recording the particulars set out in this order (and that the entry
shall be marked with the words "Convention order");

(And it is further directed that the aforesaid entry in the Register of
Births/Adopted Children Register be marked with the words "adopted"/
"readopted"/"proposed   foreign   adoption"/"proposed   foreign
readoption").

Dated this   day of   19   .

G. ORIGINATING PROCESS FOR THE ANNULMENT OR REVOCATION OF AN ADOPTION

Form 9

In the High Court
Family Division   No.   of 19

In the Matter of

and

In the Matter of the Adoption Act 1968

Let   of
attend at the Royal Courts of Justice, Strand, London WC2A 2LL on a
date to be fixed for the hearing of the application of
                                of   for an
order:—

1. That the adoption which was authorised on the
day of   19   at   , by which
              (and   ) was (*or* were)
authorised to adopt the said   be annulled (*or* revoked).

(2. That the leave of the court be granted for the purpose of making
this application out of time.)

3. That the costs of this application be provided for.

Dated this   day of   19   .

This summons was taken out by   of
              ,   solicitor for the above named
       .

Notes
   This form is for use when the adoption is to be annulled or revoked
under section 6(1) or (2) of the Adoption Act 1968. An application may
not be made unless either the adopter or both adopters, as the case
may be, or the adopted person habitually resides in Great Britain
immediately before the application is made.

Preamble. Enter the full names by which the adopted person has been known since the adoption.

Paragraph 1. Enter the description and address of the authority by which the adoption was authorised.

Paragraph 2. Except with the leave of the court, an application to annul an adoption may not be made later than two years after the date of the adoption to which it relates.

H. AGREEMENT TO AN ADOPTION ORDER/ PROPOSED FOREIGN ADOPTION

Form 7

(Heading as in Form 1)

If you are in any doubt about your legal rights you should obtain legal advice before *signing this form*

Whereas an application is to be/has been made by   and   (*or* under serial No.   ) for an adoption order or order authorising a proposed foreign adoption in respect of   a child;

And whereas the child is the person to whom the birth certificate attached marked "A" relates:

(And whereas the child is at least six weeks old:)

I, the undersigned   of   being a parent/guardian of the child hereby state as follows:

(1) I understand that the effect of an adoption order/an order authorising a proposed foreign adoption will be to deprive me permanently of the parental rights and duties relating to the child and to vest them in the applicant(s); and in particular I understand that, if an order is made, I shall have no right to see or get in touch with the child or to have him/her returned to me.

(2) I further understand that the court cannot make an adoption order/an order authorising the proposed foreign adoption of the child without the agreement of each parent or guardian of the child unless the court dispenses with an agreement on the ground that the person concerned—

    (a) cannot be found or is incapable of giving agreement, or

    (b) is withholding his agreement unreasonably, or

    (c) has persistently failed without reasonable cause to discharge the parental duties in relation to the child, or

    (d) has abandoned or neglected the child, or

    (e) has persistently ill-treated the child, or

    (f) has seriously ill-treated the child and the rehabilitation of the child within the household of the parent or guardian is unlikely.

197

(3) I further understand that when the application for an adoption order/order authorising the proposed foreign adoption of the child is heard, this document may be used as evidence of my agreement to the making of the order unless I inform the court that I no longer agree.

(4) I hereby freely, and with full understanding of what is involved, agree unconditionally to the making of an adoption order/an order authorising the proposed foreign adoption of the child in pursuance of the application.

(5) As far as I know, the only person(s) or body(ies) who has/have taken part in the arrangements for the child's adoption is/are (and   ).

(6) I have not received or given any payment or reward for, or in consideration of, the adoption of the child, for any agreement to the making of an adoption order or placing the child for adoption with any person or making arrangements for the adoption of the child (other than payment to an adoption agency for their expenses incurred in connection with the adoption).

Signature:

This form, duly completed, was signed by the said before me at   on the day of   19   .

Signature:

Address:

Description:

Appendix 4

FORMS

A. HOME OFFICE QUESTIONNAIRE TO FACILITATE ENTRY CLEARANCE

<table>
<tr>
<td>

Adoption of a child from
  overseas:
Home Office reference
  number (if known)

....

</td>
<td>

Please submit this form
and the documents
requested when you
apply for entry
clearance.

</td>
</tr>
</table>

The information requested on this form includes many of the details that will be required by a court hearing an adoption application. This form and the documents that you should enclose with it will be treated as confidential and only passed to the DH and the local authority undertaking the home study report. In some cases we may need to ask for further information.

DETAILS ABOUT THE CHILD

Surname	Date of birth
Other names	(Please enclose birth certificate
Nationality	or a signed and attested
Sex: male ☐ female ☐ (tick	statement giving the date of
one box)	birth)

Passport Number if any

Name and address of person currently looking after the child overseas:

Is this person a relative of the child?   Yes ☐   No ☐
If Yes state relationship:

Has the child attended school?   Yes ☐   No ☐
If Yes: how many years has he attended school? .... Years
        has he passed any examinations? (give details) ....

If the child has any brothers or sisters give:
names: date of birth: name of person
                                caring for them:

---

*PLEASE ATTACH A COPY OF THE MEDICAL REPORT ON THE CHILD. THIS SHOULD BE ON A BAAF FORM OBTAINABLE FROM BRITISH AGENCIES FOR ADOPTION AND FOSTERING 11 SOUTHWARK STREET LONDON SE1 1RQ (See attached annex on medical forms)

IF THE CHILD HAS BEEN CARED FOR BY A PUBLIC OR OTHER
ORGANISATION

Name and address of the body:

Date child came into their care:

DETAILS ABOUT THE CHILD'S PARENTS

	Mother	Father
Surname:		
other names;		
date of birth:		
place of birth:		
marital status:		
date of marriage:		

DETAILS ABOUT YOU

Prospective adoptive mother:
Prospective adoptive father:
Surname:
other names:
date of birth:
relationship to child:
Your home address:

Have you ever previously applied to adopt or foster a
child   ☐ Yes   ☐ No
Have you recently had a home study report
prepared?   ☐ Yes   ☐ No

If you have answered yes to either of these questions, give name
of local authority or agency or individual concerned: (Continue on
a separate sheet if necessary).

Please give the names and addresses of two personal referees
who know you both well:
        1.   2.

Please state how the child came to be offered to you for adoption?

Have you any other children? ☐ Yes   ☐ No If yes please give
                                            names and dates
                                            of birth

I certify that this information is true and correct to the best of my
knowledge.

Please sign your names here:

Undertaking by Intending Adopters

Names of intending adopters:

. . . .

. . . .

Address: . . . .

. . . .

. . . .

Home Office

Name of the child:

....

We, the undersigned agree that if entry clearance is granted for the above-named child to come to the United Kingdom for adoption by us we will, as soon as the child arrives in the United Kingdom, inform the social services department of our local authority* of our intention to apply to the court for an adoption order in respect of that child, and that we will make such application to the court.

We also agree to accept full financial responsibility for the child while the child is in the United Kingdom.

Signed: (1) ....
        (2) ....

Date: ....

* —in Northern Ireland, the Health and Social Services Board.
  —in Scotland, the Social Work Department of the Regional or Islands Council.

B. BRITISH ASSOCIATION OF ADOPTION AND FOSTERING FORM ICA

Inter-country Adoption

Medical report and developmental assessment of child under the age of 18 years

To be Completed by a Doctor in the Child's Country of Origin

NOTES FOR GUIDANCE IN USING THIS FORM

1. The form should be completed for children or young persons who are to enter the UK from another country for adoption.

2. The purpose of the form is to gather, as far as possible, the information that a doctor in the UK will require in order to write a report for the Adoption Court; to ensure that the need for any special health care is taken into account in deciding whether the proposed adoption placement is in the child's best interests; and to help those who will be caring for him or her in the UK. Its purpose is *not* to select children who would be suitable for adoption.

3. It is recognised that some of the information requested by the form may not be available in some cases. Every section of the form should be completed, and clearly marked 'not known' or 'not verified' when the information is either unavailable or uncertain.

4. It is of great importance that as much information as possible should be obtained at this stage and entered on the form. This will assist the adopters and their medical advisers to care for the child throughout childhood and will ensure that the child has some information about his or her background should he or she wish it in adulthood. By that time any information about origins would probably be very difficult to trace.

5. If space is inadequate, please continue on the back page.

CONFIDENTIAL

FORM ICA

INTER-COUNTRY ADOPTION

MEDICAL REPORT & DEVELOPMENTAL ASSESSMENT OF CHILD
UNDER 18 YEARS

Child's surname .... Forename(s) ....
Also known as .... Place, date and time of birth ....
Ethnic origin of mother .... Ethnic origin of father ....
Height and build of mother ...... Height and build of father ....
Date of examination .... Sex ....

IMPORTANT The family history on the child and his/her parents should
be available to the examining doctor.
The following information would also be helpful, and should be
attached if available:

Any previous medical report   Growth charts to date

Neonatal report/Obstetric report   List of placements   Photograph

Medical history   Any relevant specialist reports

Where these are not available, please state below *any* known information about the family history, *particularly genetic conditions in the
family*, state of health of the parents, cause of death (where appropriate), etc.

1. Period of gestation (in weeks)

2. Weight at birth

3. Head circumference at birth

4. Single or multiple birth (if
   multiple state whether first born
   or other and situation of other infant(s))

5. Were there any problems or illnesses
during this pregnancy or labour?

6. Were there any problems or illnesses of
relevance to this child in any other
pregnancies of this mother?

7. Type of delivery (*if forceps or
Caesarian please give reasons*)

8. How long after the delivery was
spontaneous respiration
established? (*If resuscitation was
required please give details*)

9. Were any abnormalities noted? eg
jaundice, convulsions, twitching

10. Were there any illnesses, abnormal occurrences
or management/feeding problems in the neo-natal
period? (*If yes, please give details*)

11. Immunisation status
(*including Bacillus Calmette Guèrin vaccination*)

12. Any other relevant information

13. PHYSICAL EXAMINATION   Date . . . . .Age . . . .

MEASUREMENTS	Weight		kgs	centile
	Height/length (if appropriate)		cms	centile
	Head circumference		cms	centile
	Blood pressure (*children 1 year and over*)			
	General appearance: *describe state of nutrition*			
	Skin/hair—any scars?			
	Mouth/state of teeth			
EARS	Examination, *including hearing*		Right	Left
EYES	Examination, *including vision and any infections*		Right	Left
	Respiratory system			
	Cardiovascular system (*including pulses*)			
	Abdomen (*including hernias*)			
	Genitalia (*including testes*)			
SKELETAL SYSTEM	Spine			
	Joints			
	Limbs			
	Hips			

NEUROLOGICAL SYSTEM	Cranial nerves	Right	Left
	Posture		
	Tone		
	Power		
	Co-ordination		
	Reflexes: Neonatal (if appropriate)		
	Tendon		
	Plantar		
	Any other observations?		

TEST RESULTS when considered advisable for the child's well-being	Date
Blood: Phenylalanine (*guthrie/other*)	
thyroid function	
full blood count	
blood film (*to exclude malaria where relevant*)	
haemoglobinopathies	
serological test for syphilis	
hepatitis B	
HIV antibody	
liver function test	
Stools: Microscopy (*to exclude parasites including giardia and amoebae*)	
Culture	
Urine	
Other	

14. DEVELOPMENTAL AND FUNCTIONAL ASSESSMENT (*taking account of caregiver's report*)

Gross motor activity
Comments (*eg any evidence of motor handicap?*)

Eye/hand function
Comments

Speech, including talking
and understanding

Social behaviour and play
Comments

(If appropriate) Does the child or young person smoke, drink alcohol or use drugs or solvents?

Does the child appear to be normal?
a) Physically
b) Mentally

15. Is there a need for follow-up
examination taking account of
previous illnesses or
symptoms (*specify if yes*)

16. Summary by examining doctor of anything in the collected information which is likely to be relevant to the child's present condition or future prospects (*e.g. genetic conditions in the family; obstetric or neonatal complications; disability; previous illnesses; accidents and operations; history of growth, development, speech and learning; frequent changes of caregiver, etc*)

17. Is the child's general health satisfactory? If not, is the child attending hospital, clinic or other special unit or receiving any medication or other treatment? List any past or current abnormal symptoms

18. Comments from person caring for child on child's health and day-to-day progress

19. Any other observations

20. Signature of examining doctor . . . .

   Name (in CAPITALS) . . . .

   Qualifications . . . .   University or Medical School . . . .

   Address . . . .

   . . . .

   Telephone . . . .   Date . . . .

21. If an adoption agency is involved with this child, either in the country of origin or in the UK, please give particulars.

   Adoption agency . . . .

   Address . . . .

   . . . .

   Social worker . . . .   Telephone . . . .

   Country . . . .

   Medical adviser (if any) . . . .

   Telephone . . . .

C. MEDICAL REPORT ON PROSPECTIVE ADOPTIVE/FOSTER PARENT

Form Adult 1

Agency details   Name of agency

Address	Social worker
	Telephone
	Medical adviser
Postcode Telephone	Telephone

Applicant	Surname	Forename(s)
	Address	Date of birth
		Occupation
		Case reference number

The information recorded on this form will be of great importance in decisions regarding the future placement of a child. If you have any points of concern in completing the form, please contact the medical adviser as shown above.

CONSENT

I understand that information about my medical history and present medical condition is required by the above-named agency. I consent to a medical examination, to the provision of this report to the agency and to any further enquiries deemed necessary.

Signature of applicant

1

To be completed by the examining doctor

Are you the applicant's usual attendant? If not explain current role.

How long have you been his/her doctor?

At what date do your records begin?

When and for what purpose did he/she last consult you?

Is he/she currently receiving any medication or other treatment? If yes please specify.

213

2   **Family history of applicant**

		Living State of Health	Dead Cause of death and date
Father	Age		
Mother			
Siblings	Sex		
Children (include and indicate with an asterisk any adopted children)—			

Is there any history of hereditary conditions in the family?

3 Medical history

Is there any history (medical, surgical or traumatic) referable to the following systems?

Please give details (including treatments, dates and duration) or write NONE

Blood and haematopoietic system

Cardiovascular system

Respiratory system (including nose and throat)

Digest system

Nervous system

Special senses: vision

hearing

Urogenital system (for females include details of any pregnancies)

Glandular system (including diabetes, endocrines, breasts and lymph nodes)

Musculo-skeletal system

Skin

4 What is the daily consumption of:

Cigarettes/   Alcohol   Habit forming drugs
tobacco

5   Examination data

Measurements   Height   ft/ins   or   cms

Weight   (in   light   stones/lbs   or   kgs
clothes)

(Tick for normal in box or enter finding in right hand column as appropriate)

Blood and haematopoietic system

       Anaemia?   ☐

Cardiovascular system

Resting blood pressure* systolic/   ☐ 1st recording*   ☐ 2nd recording*   ☐ 3rd recording*
diastolic (5th Phase)
*If raised please repeat after an interval
and enter in spaces provided   →

       Pulse   →   Rate   Rhythm

       Heart: size   ☐

             sounds   ☐

           murmurs?   ☐

       Varicose veins?   ☐

       Optic fundi   ☐

Respiratory system   Trachea   ☐

       Chest shape   ☐
       Percussion   ☐
       Breath sounds   ☐
       Other signs?

Result and date of chest X-ray

(if indicated by clinical history, examination or local conditions)

Digestive system   Mouth   ☐
                 Abdomen   ☐
                 Liver   ☐
                 Spleen   ☐
                 Hernia?   ☐

Nervous system   Cranial nerves   ☐
              Limb tone   ☐
              Tremor?   ☐
              Reflexes   ☐
              Co-ordination   ☐
              Sensation   ☐
              Other signs?

Special senses   Vision   ☐
             Hearing   ☐

Urogenital system Any abnormality?   ☐

       Urine tests (essential) → Albumin?   Sugar?   Blood?

Glandular system   Breasts   ☐
               Lymph nodes   ☐

Musculo-skeletal   Spine   ☐
system

Limbs	☐	
Joints	☐	

Skin ☐

6   Is any other opinion or investigation required?

7   Marital history

Duration of marriage

Any previous marriage?

Is natural parenthood contra-indicated? Why?

Is any family   contraception?
limitation due to: sterilisation?
                      failure to conceive?

If 'failure to conceive' give duration and reason. Please specify investigations and any treatments.

8   Mental health

Does the applicant have any history of psychiatric disorder?
(This includes depression, other neurotic conditions, personality disorders and psychoses)

Has he/she had any psychiatric treatment? (Specify and give dates)

Does he/she have any emotional/relationship problems?

If there have been psychiatric/emotional problems, how would you assess the applicant's:

               present condition?

               long-term prognosis?

9 Opinion of examining doctor

Please comment on the ability of this applicant to care adequately for a child until the age of independence (See covering letter for deatils of any particular child(ren) being considered)

Signed   Name (in CAPITALS)

Address   Telephone

                                          Date

To be completed by the agency medical adviser

Comment on the significance of this report for adoption/fostering

Signature

                                          Date

Appendix 5

CASE DIGEST

RE A (A MINOR) (WARDSHIP: IMMIGRATION)

[1992] I F.L.R. 427

IMMIGRATION ... WARDSHIP ... CITIZENS OF BANGLADESH MARRYING AND HAVING CHILD IN UNITED KINGDOM ... MOTHER LAWFULLY RESIDENT ... FATHER NOT ... WARDSHIP PROCEEDINGS BROUGHT

The Facts

The mother, a Bangladeshi citizen, came to the United Kingdom in 1987 when she was 16 to join her parents. She was allowed entry for the purpose of settlement. The father was also a citizen of Bangladesh and he was admitted into the United Kingdom for one month in 1988 to visit his brother. The couple married 10 days later and the father applied for leave to remain on the ground of his marriage. Such leave was refused on the ground he entered by deception and was consequently considered to be an illegal immigrant. It was decided in May 1990 that he be sent back to Bangladesh despite a child being born to the couple in June 1989. Wardship proceedings were therefore commenced in October 1990 seeking for the child to be warded with care and control being committed to the parents, and with her not being removed from the jurisdiction without the leave of the court. The parents appealed the court's refusal to continue keeping the child a ward on the application of the Secretary of State for the Home Office.

Held

The appeal was dismissed. The child was in the care and control of her parents who were not in dispute about her. The only reason for the wardship application had been to fetter the Secretary of State regarding the immigration status of the father. Only he could decide upon the Father's immigration status by reason of the decision-making power granted him by Parliament. Fettering this discretion was against public policy and an abuse of the court's process.

RE A (ADOPTION: PLACEMENT)

[1988] 1 W.L.R. 229; [1988] 2 F.L.R. 133; (1988) 18 Fam. Law 293

ADOPTION ORDER MADE OUTSIDE UNITED KINGDOM . . . ADOP-
TION AGENCY IN UNITED STATES . . . ADOPTION OF CHILD IN EL
SALVADOR . . . WHETHER CHILD PLACED OUTSIDE OR INSIDE
JURISDICTION

The Facts

An adoption agency in the United States organised the adoption of a
child in El Salvador. The applicants in England consulted the Home
Office and on being informed that the adoption order in El Salvador
could not create a valid adoptive relationship, they promised to begin
proceedings in England, promising the court of El Salvador the same.
The child met the applicants at Heathrow having passed through
customs and immigration. The matter came before the county court
which transferred it to the High Court on the ground there had been a
breach of section 29(1) of the Adoption Act 1958 in that no person
other than an approved adoption agency should place a child for
adoption, unless the proposed adopters are relatives or acting in
pursuance of a High Court order. The adopters sought to have the
registrar's order set aside, saying that as the placement occurred
outside of the jurisdiction, the section did not apply. It was suggested
that in any case, the court should allow the adoption to proceed.

Held

Whilst section 29 had no extra-territorial effect, the placement for
adoption had taken place within the jurisdiction when the child was
handed over for adoption at Heathrow. That caused a breach of
section 29 in that the proposed adopter was not a relative of the child
and was not acting in pursuance of an order of the High Court. Only
the High Court could authorise the making of arrangements by a
person other than an adoption agency. That power was exercised and
the matter then returned to the county court.

RE A (AN INFANT)

[1963] 1 W.L.R. 231; [1963] 1 All E.R. 531

ADOPTION . . . INFANT ALIEN AGED 20 YEARS . . . QUESTION OF DISCRETION

The Facts

A married couple sought to adopt a French boy born in 1942. The boy's father had died soon after his birth and he had been adopted by his mother's step-father under French law. He had lived with his mother until 1952 but was then educated at boarding schools in England, visiting his mother during school holidays. The boy and his mother had temporary permits to live in England. The boy was the second cousin of the male applicant and was a trainee in a company of which the male applicant was a director at the time of the application. He went to live with the applicants and their children in July 1962 to fulfill the conditions prescribed by section 3(1) of the Adoption Act 1958. The object of the adoption was to enable him to acquire British nationality under section 19(1) of the Adoption Act 1958.

Held

Where a person to be adopted is 19 or 20 years of age the wording in the Act, namely "care and possession" would bear an artificial meaning but they at least do require the applicants, with whom the person is living to be *in loco parentis* to him. This was not considered to be the position regarding the boy. Such an adoption could be objected to on the grounds of public policy because an alien infant, for example, could arrange to be adopted in England, to carry out some undesirable activity, whilst putting forward a plausible case to the judge. The court would then be taking on a role similar to that of the Home Secretary on an application for naturalisation. The order was refused.

RE ADOPTION APPLICATION (ADOPTION OF NON-PATRIAL)

[1992] 1 W.L.R. 596; [1992] 1 F.L.R. 341; [1992] Fam. Law 241

ADOPTION OF FOREIGN CHILD . . . CHILD BROUGHT TO ENGLAND FROM EL SALVADOR . . . CRIMINAL PROCEEDINGS PENDING AGAINST APPLICANT . . . ADOPTION IN CHILD'S INTEREST

The Facts

Knowing they were unable to adopt through English agencies by reason of their age, the applicants (who had had one child themselves), commissioned a home study report from the local authority, paying £200 with a view to adopt a foreign child. The husband was charged in August 1988 with criminal activities. He was a solicitor. The applicants were notified by their lawyers in El Salvador of the birth of a girl in April 1989. Adoption papers were prepared for them with a notarial document signifying the natural mother's consent. On receipt of them the husband flew to El Salvador, returning with the baby, the wife meeting them at Heathrow. The local authority social services were then notified of their wish to adopt. The formal adoption order was made by the court in El Salvador on September 21, 1989, followed by a notarial confirmation of the natural mother's consent. Neither the local authority or the court of El Salvador knew of the husband's impending criminal proceedings. He was in fact imprisoned for four years in February 1990 for obtaining property by deception. He was released on parole in August 1991. The Guardian *ad litem*, whilst accepting at the adoption application that the baby had bonded to the wife and her son, opposed the adoption. She said it would not be in the child's best interest because of the background and behaviour of the husband; that the breaches of the Adoption Act 1976 precluded her agreement; and that an order should not be made for reasons of public policy. The local authority did criticise the attitude of the husband and the wife but believed it was in the child's best interest for the adoption to go ahead.

Held

The behaviour of the applicants did not justify removing the child from them since the child should not be faced with further disruptions. Although the applicants might not have been accepted for an application for a British child or for a child from overseas, the matter became less relevant after placement as the *de facto* situation had to be considered.

Whilst the placement of the child with the wife at Heathrow constituted an "arrangement for the adoption of a child made by a person other than an adoption agency," contravening section II(I) of the Adoption Act 1976, the High Court could grant its dispensation to enable the adoption to take place. Authorisation could also be granted retrospectively regarding payment or reward. Ultimately, considerations of the child's welfare outweighed public policy, so the court should use its powers of dispensation and grant the order.

Any local authority advised of a child's arrival from abroad for adoption should seek information from a relevant embassy to the validity of the foreign adoption order obtained.

RE ARIF (AN INFANT); RE SINGH (AN INFANT)

[1968] 2 W.L.R. 1290; [1968] 2 All E.R. 145

WARDSHIP JURISDICTION . . . COMMONWEALTH CITIZEN . . . ADMISSION TO UNITED KINGDOM REFUSED.

The Facts

(1) A, a boy aged about 11 and a citizen of Pakistan arrived at London airport. If the boy was under 16 years of age and the plaintiff's son, as claimed, he would have been entitled to admission, as the plaintiff was a United Kingdom resident. The immigration officer was dissatisfied after questioning the boy and the plaintiff regarding whether he was indeed the plaintiff's son and refused admission under section 2(1) of the Commonwealth Immigrants Act 1962 and arrangements were made for him to be returned to Pakistan.

(2) NS was an Indian aged 17 who arrived at London airport with a lady and a girl said to be his mother and sister. HS, who was resident in England, alleged that NS was his son. The immigration officer after due inquiries was dissatisfied. He was refused admission and arrangements were also made for NS's return.

The plaintiffs both issued an originating summons seeking to make A and NS wards of court.

Held

The court would not exercise wardship jurisdiction to interfere with the statutory immigration controls. There was a comprehensive code governing the entry or removal of Commonwealth immigrants entrusted to good administration by immigration officers which, so long as the statutory control was honestly and fairly exercised, would not be interfered with.

RE A W (ADOPTION APPLICATION)

[1993] 1 F.L.R. 62; [1992] Fam. Law 539

ADOPTERS PAYING TO ASSIST IN ADOPTION . . . ADOPTION HEARING FOUR-AND-A-HALF YEARS AFTER PLACEMENT

The Facts

The child in question was born in 1987. The applicants had already adopted in 1980 after a private placement not at that time prevented. They were 60 and 62 respectively and they knew by reason of health, age and problems within their marriage they would not be regarded as suitable. They decided deliberately to get around the law. They arranged with a pregnant English woman who did not want to keep her baby for her to have it in Germany and paid £1,000 towards her expenses in England and hospital costs in Germany. They hid the facts from the local authority, hoping that by the time they might be found out the child would have been with them for so long that the removal could not be considered realistically. The local authority failed to discharge their duty under the Adoption Rules 1984.

Held

Section 11 of the Adoption Act 1976 provides that no person other than an adoption agency should place a child for adoption unless the applicant was a relative of the child or he was acting in accordance with an order of the High Court. Under section 57 of the 1976 Act there was to be no financial provision to bring about an adoption. The payment of moneys to the natural mother was plainly wrong and in considering whether dispensation should be granted to remedy breaches there was a balancing exercise between public policy and the welfare of the child. The welfare of the child demanded he should remain within the family in that he was settled and receiving love as well as a good standard of care. However, the behaviour of the applicants and their health caused anxiety. The deliberate manipulation of the system by the applicants could be said to be contrary to public policy but the child's welfare outweighed public policy. The breaches were authorised and an interim order was made under section 25 of the 1976 Act, vesting legal authority in the applicants for a probationary period of not more than two years, under which the guardian and local authority were to be provided with reports every six months.

RE B (S) (AN INFANT)

[1968] Ch. 204; [1967] 3 W.L.R. 1438; [1967] 3 All E.R. 629

ADOPTION . . . FOREIGN ELEMENT . . . DOMICILE . . . RECOGNI-
TION BY SPAIN OF ENGLISH ADOPTION ORDER . . . JURISDICTION

The Facts

A married couple sought an adoption order in the county court
regarding the legitimate daughter of an English mother and Spanish
father, domiciled in Spain in that the matrimonial home was in Spain
although the mother had left the father and returned to England. She
then found out that she was pregnant and decided to have the child
adopted. She placed the child with the married couple when it was
eight days old. The Spanish father's consent to the adoption order had
not been obtained and the judge dismissed the application to dispense
with consent on the ground that consent had not been unreasonably
withheld. The judge's decision was upheld on appeal. The mother then
petitioned for divorce, seeking residency of the child as well. The father
made no appearance and the mother obtained a decree absolute and
a residency order.
The proposed adopters sought an order that father's consent should
be dispensed with, on the ground this time that he had persistently
failed without reasonable cause to discharge the obligations of a
parent (Adoption Act 1958, s.5). The father received notice in Spain
but made no acknowledgement, did not attend the hearing and made
no representations.

Held

The English court did have jurisdiction over a child resident within the
jurisdiction, even if domiciled abroad, irrespective of the consequences elsewhere of an order made in exercise of that jurisdiction
as the provisions of domicile in the Adoption Act 1958 were directed
solely to the proposed adopters. However, the consequence of foreign
law had to be considered since it could be disadvantageous to a child
to have one status in one country and another in another country.
Ultimately, it was a matter of the child's welfare and the English court
was satisfied that the court in Spain would recognise an English order.

Considering the evidence in itself, the Spanish father had done nothing to discharge his parental obligations, so his consent to the adoption could be dispensed with.

RE C (MINORS: ADOPTION BY RELATIVE)

[1989] 1 W.L.R. 61; [1989] 1 All E.R. 395; [1989] 1 F.L.R. 222

REMOVAL OF CHILD FROM GREAT BRITAIN . . . WHETHER GREAT UNCLE A RELATIVE . . . WARDSHIP JURISDICTION

The Facts

The parents' marriage broke down and the children were made wards of court and committed to the care of the local authority, who were given leave to place them with foster parents with a view to adoption. The paternal great aunt and uncle of the children, who were domiciled in Australia, wanted to adopt them and they were regarded as suitable by the local authority. An application was made for leave to remove the children from the jurisdiction. Within section 56(1) of the Adoption Act 1976 removal for adoption outside Great Britain by any person not a parent or guardian or relative of the child was prohibited so the authority sought a declaration that the great-uncle was a relative or alternatively sought an order that the great aunt or uncle were the children's guardians. The judge would not consider them as relatives but did make them guardians of the children pending the hearing of the application for them to be removed from the jurisdiction. The natural mother was opposed to the application by the great-uncle and aunt and appealed the court order with the authority cross-appealing against the order that a great-uncle was not a relative.

Held

The court had regard to section 72(1) of the Adoption Act 1976 which considered an uncle but not a great uncle as a great-uncle was not a relative. It was also considered doubtful whether the court had inherent jurisdiction to make a guardianship order where wardship was existing because it derogated from the jurisdiction of wardship and the statutory powers belonging to a local authority regarding the care of the children. The mother's appeal against the interim order was therefore allowed.

RE F (A MINOR) (IMMIGRATION; WARDSHIP)

[1989] 3 W.L.R. 691; [1989] 1 All E.R. 1155; [1990] Fam. 125; [1989] 1 F.L.R. 233

WARD . . . IMMIGRATION . . . CHILD BROUGHT INTO UNITED KING-DOM . . . OVERSTAYING LEAVE TO ENTER . . . LIABLE TO BE REMOVED . . . WHETHER WARDSHIP JURISDICTION WOULD AFFECT IMMIGRATION AUTHORITY

The Facts

The child was born in Nigeria in April 1981. His father died in July 1982 and nothing was known about his mother. He was brought to England by his aunt in August 1992 on her passport and was granted leave to enter as a visitor for six months. He was placed with foster parents under an informal arrangement with the consent of the local authority. His uncle sent money to the foster parents for his upkeep and then he went to visit his uncle in Nigeria. On his return in January 1987 it was discovered that he had overstayed his six-month leave but was granted temporary admission while inquiries were made. He returned to his foster parents who were unaware of any restriction on his entry, but made him a ward of court once they became aware of it. The wardship summons was struck out on the application of the Secretary of State as an abuse of process, so the foster parents then appealed, with the Secretary of State agreeing not to remove the child until the determination of the adoption proceedings.

Held

It was held to be an abuse of process to use wardship proceedings to keep within the country a child who had overstayed his leave to enter. By impeding the immigration authorities in exercising their statutory power to remove the child, it would fetter the discretion of Parliament. There would be some cases where the use of wardship was acceptable for the welfare of the child pending consideration of his position. The court would allow the child to be a ward of court until further order, namely the consideration of the adoption, and to that extent the appeal would be allowed.

RE H (A MINOR) (ADOPTION: NON-PATRIAL)

[1982] 3 W.L.R. 501; [1982] 3 All E.R. 84

ADOPTION . . . UNCLE AND AUNT WISHING TO ADOPT . . . IMMI-GRATION AUTHORITIES REGARDING ADOPTION AS CIRCUMVENT-ING IMMIGRATION CONTROL

The Facts

A Pakistani boy aged 14 had been given leave to enter the United Kingdom in December 1978 on a month's visitor's visa to visit his grandparents and his uncle and aunt, the applicants. The boy had been rejected by his family in Pakistan having been turned out of his home in September 1978. In January 1979 the applicants made an application for an extension to stay and decided that the best solution would be to adopt the boy. In April 1979 notice of intention to adopt had been given to the local authority and the Home Office. The latter refused the initial application for an extension to stay on the ground that the boy was not thought to be a genuine visitor. On appeal it was decided by the Secretary of State that there had been no genuine transfer of parental responsibility and that the adoption application was one of convenience to enable the boy to remain in the country. In August 1980 adoption proceedings were initiated.

Held

The court could make an adoption order notwithstanding the adverse decision of the immigration authorities. In reaching a decision regarding the adoption of a child, the court should have regard to all the circumstances, the first being the need to safeguard and promote the welfare of the child throughout his childhood. Where the minor was approaching majority and was a foreign national the court should pay great regard to the immigration decision and must be aware of the possibility of abuse of the adoption process. The fact that nationality or partiality might result should not be conclusive to the final decision. The court was satisfied that the applicants had a genuine wish for the sake of the boy to keep him as a member of the family and were in actual custody of him. There was a genuine transfer of parental responsibility and so the application was not one of convenience. If he were returned to Pakistan he would have no home to go to as his family had indeed rejected him and it would be harsh and illogical to reject the application on the ground that he would soon attain his majority. The welfare considerations prevailed.

RE K (A MINOR) (ADOPTION ORDER: NATIONALITY)

[1994] 3 W.L.R. 572; *The Times,* April 26, 1994

ADOPTION APPLICATION . . . CHILD REACHING MAJORITY BY THE TIME OF APPEAL . . . WHETHER APPLICATION FOR ADOPTION WAS A SUBSTITUTE FOR IMMIGRATION APPLICATION

The Facts

The child was born in Sierra Leone and brought up by her mother who had died in 1988. The aunt had adopted her in Sierra Leone in 1991 and the child had then flown to London and gained temporary admission without entry clearance. The aunt had applied to adopt the child in England with the support of the Official Solicitor acting as Guardian *ad litem.* The Home Secretary had opposed the adoption. The High Court allowed the adoption and the matter was appealed. The child had reached her majority before the notice of the appeal had been served and the Court of Appeal believed that the Official Solicitor no longer had *locus standi,* although he was invited to remain as *amicus curiae.*

Held

It was common ground that the court was entitled to take into account benefits accruing to the child after the age of 18 other than those derived from her status as a British national. A finding that the applicant's motive was to achieve nationality and the right of abode for the child rather than serve her general welfare was to rule the application out of court. If the court was satisfied that that was not the motive, it could then commence a balancing exercise between public policy and the child's welfare. The benefits accruing to the child from adoption were minimal as compared to the aspect of public policy in relation to the effect of the adoption order on nationality itself and her right of abode. The adoption order had no practical consequences for the child's welfare. A court having to decide upon an adoption order that would automatically grant British citizenship must consider the substance of the position. An adoption application could not be a substitute for an immigration application. The appeal was allowed.

RE M (AN INFANT) (ADOPTION: CHILD'S REMOVAL FROM JURISDICTION)

[1973] 2 W.L.R. 515; [1973] 1 All E.R. 852; [1973] Fam. 66

PROVISIONAL ADOPTION BY PERSON RESIDENT OUTSIDE GREAT BRITAIN . . . PROSPECTIVE ADOPTERS MAKING CHILD A WARD OF COURT

The Facts

The applicants were of Danish nationality, domiciled and resident in Denmark. They wished to adopt an illegitimate girl, aged two, who was in the care of a local authority and was living with foster parents in England. The applicants made the child a ward of court, simultaneously seeking to remove her from the jurisdiction so that they might have continuous care and control of her for six months as required by sections 3(1) and 53(5) of the Adoption Act 1958 before applying to the court for a provisional adoption order. The question remained as to whether the court was able to grant leave for the child's removal, as section 52(1) of the Adoption Act 1958 prevented removal "to any place outside the British Islands with a view to adoption of the infant." The applicants submitted that the removal would not be with a view to adopting the child, but only with a view to returning the child to England after six months to apply for a provisional adoption order. The child being a ward of court, they also submitted that the court could make it a condition of granting leave that the applicants provide guarantees and undertakings for her due return to England.

Held

The application was dismissed because there was a prohibition of removal under the Act with a view to a British child's adoption, except under the authority of a provisional adoption order. The expression, "with a view to adoption" was a broad and comprehensive expression where the removal was a step in a larger process the ultimate purpose of which was indeed adoption. Although the child was a ward of court, it was irrelevant that the court could grant permission for removal subject to undertakings or guarantees.

MATHIEU v. ENTRY CLEARANCE OFFICER, BRIDGETOWN

[1979-1980] Imm. A.R. 157

OVERSEAS ADOPTION . . . ADOPTION VALID UNDER LAW OF ST LUCIA WHERE ADOPTION ORDER MADE . . . NOT AN OVERSEAS ADOPTION UNDER UNITED KINGDOM STATUTORY LAW . . . WHETHER ELIGIBILITY FOR SETTLEMENT PRECLUDED IF ADOPTION NOT DESIGNATED OVERSEAS ADOPTION

The Facts

The appellants appealed to the Immigration Appeal Tribunal against the determination of the adjudicator dismissing their appeals against the refusal to grant them entry to the United Kingdom for settlement as the adopted children of Mr and Mrs Mathieu. The appellants at the time of the refusal were citizens of the United Kingdom, Associated States and Colonies and Mr and Mrs Mathieu were citizens of the United Kingdom, Associated States and Colonies but living in and settled in the United Kingdom. Mr Mathieu had been ordinarily resident in the United Kingdom since 1961 and claimed to be the natural father of the three appellants, with Lucia and Raymond, two of the children, having one mother, Michael, another.

In 1974 Mr Mathieu obtained orders from the High Court of St Lucia whereby he and his wife adopted all three children. The entry clearance officer heard that another man also claimed to be the father of Michael, with Michael's mother confirming this. The records showed that Michael was the legitimate son of a Mr and Mrs Joseph and Mr and Mrs Joseph had not consented to the adoption of Michael despite the Adoption Ordinance of St Lucia 1954 stating that natural parents must give their consent. There had been no genuine transfer of parental responsibility and the adoption could be construed simply to have facilitated entry into the United Kingdom. The entry clearance officer refused the applications regarding all three children because Mr and Mrs Mathieu were not seen by him to be parents for the purposes of paragraph 43(a) of the statement of changes to the Immigration Rules (H.C. 79). The definition of parent is extended to include an adoptive parent but only where there has been a genuine transfer of parental responsibility on the ground of the original parents' inability to care for the child.

Held

It was not necessary for a child to be legally adopted as defined in section 33(1) of the Immigration Act 1971, namely that the adoption be

236

specified as an overseas adoption by order of the Secretary of State under section 4(3) of the Adoption Act 1968. However, on the facts of the case, the appeal was dismissed because it was thought that the adoption was indeed one of convenience arranged to facilitate the children's admission to the United Kingdom.

RE N AND L (MINORS) (ADOPTION PROCEEDINGS: VENUE)

[1987] 1 W.L.R. 829; [1987] 2 All E.R. 732; [1988] 1 F.L.R. 48

TRANSFER OF PROCEEDINGS BETWEEN HIGH AND COUNTY COURT . . . ISSUES OF COMPLEXITY, DIFFICULTY OR GRAVITY

The Facts

A husband and wife were prospective adopters and appealed an order of the Circuit Judge who had upheld the decision of the Registrar directing that two relevant actions be transferred to the Principal Registry under section 39 of the Matrimonial and Family Proceedings Act 1984. The two children were Chilean, the elder of whom was taken into the care of the applicants when nine days old. They were authorised to remove her by order of the Chilean court who also gave them tutorship (guardianship) of her. The younger girl was taken into their care when about one-month old and they were similarly granted tutorship and leave to remove her. The applicants brought the children to England with the consent of the Home Office and also notified their local authority.

The Registrar described the case as being simple when first hearing the application but decided that by reason of the *Practice Direction* dated April 28, 1986, he had no choice but to transfer the case to the Principal Registry of the Family Division.

Held

If an application for adoption resulting in the acquisition by a child of British nationality has been launched in the county court, and it appears to that court that by reason of complexity, difficulty or gravity of issues they ought to be tried in the High Court, a case would nevertheless be suitable triable in a county court where issues of fact and law are in fact straightforward, easy and lightweight. If such cases prove at a later stage to be complex, difficult or grave then it would always be open to the county court to transfer the proceedings to the High Court. The appeal would be allowed.

PATEL v. VISA OFFICER BOMBAY

[1990] Imm. A.R. 297

DEED OF ADOPTION IN INDIA . . . WHETHER RECOGNISED UNDER ENGLISH LAW . . . WHETHER OVERSEAS ADOPTION RECOGNISED BY COMMON LAW . . . QUESTION OF DOMICILE . . . WHETHER *DE FACTO* ADOPTION

The Facts

The appellant was an Indian citizen, adopted in India by an aunt and uncle who were both resident in the United Kingdom. An application made in Bombay for entry clearance for her to join her adoptive parents was dismissed. It was argued that the deed of adoption in India should be recognised or, in the alternative, that the adoption was valid under common law. Unfortunately, the sponsors, namely, the aunt and uncle, had not taken over all responsibilities for the appellant, including those of a day to day nature to the exclusion of the parents, nor had the appellant been living with the sponsors as an integral part of the family for any substantial period of time.

Held

The adoption could not be an overseas adoption as India was not a recognised country under the Adoption Act 1976. In terms of a common law adoption, *Re Valentine's Settlement* (see below for the facts of this case) was relied upon in that it had been held that the adoption order of a foreign court would not be recognised under English law unless the adopting applicants were domiciled in the country of the court making the order. Nor can there be said to have been a *de facto* adoption. Whilst there was a genuine transfer of parental responsibility, the applicant did remain with her natural parents and they did appear to treat her as their own daughter irrespective of the passing of the date of the deed of adoption. The reality of the adoption was that the aunt and uncle could not of themselves have a child; it was never a case of the natural parents being unable to care for their daughter. It was doubtful whether the appellant could make a claim under section 1(5) of the Immigration Act 1971 or under the Commonwealth Immigrants Act 1962 and 1968. Under those statutes a child under 16 had a right of entry and child included an adopted child. However, that issue was never properly

239

decided as it was held that there had simply been a failure to establish a *de facto* adoption. Nor, finally, was it shown that there was any serious and compelling family or other considerations which made the exclusion of the appellant undesirable.

PRACTICE DIRECTION (INTERCOUNTRY ADOPTIONS: TRANSFER OF PROCEEDINGS)

[1994] 1 W.L.R. 13; [1994] Fam. Law 19

In proceedings in a county court under the Adoption Act 1976 concerning a child whose place of origin is outside the United Kingdom, the question of transfer of the case to the High Court may arise. In deciding whether, under the Children (Allocation of Proceedings) Order 1991, such proceedings are appropriate for determination in the High Court, guidance may continue to be derived from the decision of the Court of Appeal in *Re N and L (Minors) (Adoption Proceedings: Venue)* [1987] 1 W.L.R. 829, that transfer should be limited to those cases giving rise to issues of complexity, difficulty or gravity.

Orders for transfer should not be made of the court's own motion without the parties and the Guardian *ad litem* (if appointed) having the opportunity of making representations on the question of transfer. It will usually be possible for the necessary inquiries to be made by letter and for the matter to be determined without a hearing. In those cases where there is an issue as to transfer, a hearing for determination of the issue should be fixed, with notice of the date, time and place of hearing given to the parties and the Guardian *ad litem*. It will usually be impracticable to obtain the views of the natural parents or for them to be given notice of any hearing.

Issued with the approval of the President and the concurrence of the Lord Chancellor.

RE R (ADOPTION)

[1967] 1 W.L.R. 34; [1966] 3 All E.R. 613

ADOPTION . . . DISPENSATION WITH PARENTAL CONSENT . . . CHILD'S UNCORROBORATED EVIDENCE OF THEIR INDIFFERENCE TO HIS FATE . . . ABANDONMENT . . . PARENTS CANNOT BE FOUND OR INCAPABLE OF GIVING CONSENT

The Facts

R aged 20, a refugee, escaped to England and then lived with A as a member of A's family who assumed financial responsibility including payment of educational fees for him. A was both domiciled and resident in England and had children of a similar age to R. R's parents were left in the country from where he came and, whilst not sympathetically looked upon by the authorities there, had still been at liberty when R had left. The judge had accepted R's evidence of his parents' lack of curiosity when he had told them he wished to leave. They had seemed passive and indifferent altogether. It had also been accepted that R did not intend to return to his country of origin, as this would place his life at risk. R only had a temporary permit to remain in England but if adopted would become a British subject and would obviously be entitled to remain. Both R and A conceded this as attractive but also believed that were R to become a part of A's family, then it would have benefits psychologically and sociologically for R. Notice of the proceedings had not been served upon the natural parents and there remained the problem of their consent.

Held

The court could dispense with their consent as it had a discretion to override the Adoption Rules in this circumstance. Whilst R's parents might not have abandoned their son, they could not be found and were incapable of giving their consent. Since A was *in loco parentis* to R, the court would exercise its discretion in making an adoption order subject to the acceptance by the Home Office that there were no security anxieties which they might think ought to be brought to the court's attention before an order was made.

R. v. IMMIGRATION APPEAL TRIBUNAL, ex p. ALI

[1988] 2 F.L.R. 523; (1989) 133 S.J. 1002; [1988] Imm. A.R. 237; (1988) 18 Fam. Law 289

APPLICANT SEEKING ENTRY INTO JURISDICTION AS ADOPTIVE SON OF SPONSOR . . . APPLICANT AND SPONSOR RELATED . . . WHETHER ADOPTIVE PARENT WITHIN IMMIGRATION RULES . . . WHETHER LEGALLY RECOGNISED ADOPTIVE PROCESS

The Facts

In 1975 the sponsor, who had settled in the United Kingdom, visited Bangladesh and met the applicant who was born there in 1969. They were related. The applicant's mother disappeared during the visit and it was the dying father's wish that the sponsor be responsible for the son. When the father died the applicant was taken into the sponsor's family home. There was no legally recognisable adoptive process in Bangladesh or under Islamic law. In 1982 the applicant applied under paragraph 50 of the statement of changes to the Immigration Rules (H.C. 169) for an entry certificate to enable him to settle in the United Kingdom as the dependent adopted son of the sponsor. Paragraph 50 stated that unmarried children under 18 were to be admitted for settlement if one parent or a relative other than a parent was settled in the United Kingdom and that parent included an adoptive parent where there had been a genuine transfer of parental responsibility and where the adoption was not one of convenience to ease the admission of the child. The entry clearance officer refused entry in 1983 and the appeal was dismissed by the adjudicator in 1984. A further appeal was dismissed by the Immigration Appeal Tribunal in 1985; but that decision was quashed in 1986 on an application for judicial review. The Immigration Appeal Tribunal appealed to the Court of Appeal.

Held

The appeal was dismissed. It was said that whether the adoption was legal or *de facto* the immigration authorities had to decide whether there had been a genuine transfer of parental responsibility or not and whether the adoption was one of convenience to facilitate the child's admission. Since the applicant was related to the sponsor, the tribunal had been wrong in failing to consider the application of paragraph 50

243

regarding a "relative other than a parent" if it was not satisfied that the sponsor was an adoptive parent.

R. v. IMMIGRATION APPEAL TRIBUNAL, ex p. SINGH

[1988] Imm. A.R. 510; [1989] C.O.D. 204; [1989] 1 F.L.R. 115; [1989] Fam. Law 110

FORMAL ADOPTION BY AUNT OF NEPHEW . . . BURDEN OF PROOF

The Facts

The applicant had been adopted in accordance with Hindu law by his aunt who was childless and divorced. The adoption took place because of the aunt's fear of looking after herself in old age. After the adoption the child was left in the family home in India, being cared for by grandparents. Entry clearance was refused. On appeal the adjudicator held that the adoption had not been shown to have taken place because of the inability of the original parents to care for the child, and that it was for the applicant to prove they were not able to care for him. It was submitted to the court that once the formal and genuine nature of the adoption had been established the burden of proof lay on the Secretary of State to show that the other requirements of the Immigration Rules had not been established.

Held

It was always for the applicants to show that all requirements of the Immigration Rules were satisfied. The Court of Appeal held that it would be impossible for the Secretary of State to discharge that burden of proof if it were laid on him. The applicant had to show he was an adoptive child and that there had been a genuine transfer of parental responsibility on the ground of the original parents' inability to care. He also had to show that the purpose of the adoption was not to facilitate entry into the United Kingdom.

R. v. SECRETARY OF STATE FOR THE HOME DEPARTMENT, ex p. BRASSEY AND ANOTHER

[1989] 2 F.L.R. 486; [1989] Imm. A.R. 258; [1989] Fam. Law 356; (1989) 133 S.J. 388

APPLICANT SEEKING BRITISH PASSPORT . . . RELYING ON ADOPTION BY BRITISH SUBJECT LIVING ABROAD . . . APPLICATION REJECTED . . . JUDICIAL REVIEW OF WHETHER ADOPTION GRANTED BRITISH NATIONALITY

The Facts

The applicant was born of South African parentage in Switzerland in 1947. The British Nationality Act came into force on January 1,1949. His parents divorced in 1949 and his mother married a British subject who adopted the applicant under the Children's Act 1937 of South Africa. The applicant applied for a British passport to British Consulate-General in Johannesburg and his wife sought registration as a British citizen. The applications were rejected and judicial review sought.

Held

Judicial review was not granted. When the British Nationality Act 1948 came into force, the applicant did not have a British father. At the relevant date, therefore, there were no facts establishing any legal relationship between the applicant and his adoptive father and his natural father was not a British subject. A change of nationality was provided by the Adoption of Children Act 1949 and the Adoption Act 1976, but it took effect from the date of the adoption order and not the date of birth. The applicant did not have any rights other than those under statute, since the common law did not acknowledge the adoption.

R. v. SECRETARY OF STATE FOR HOME DEPART-MENT, ex p. KHAN

[1984] 1 W.L.R. 1337; [1985] 1 All E.R. 40; [1984] Imm. A.R. 68

SECRETARY OF STATE'S CIRCULAR ... SETTING OUT CRITERIA AND PROCEDURE ... ENTRY OF CHILD FOR ADOPTION ... WHETHER CIRCULAR CREATING LEGITIMATE EXPECTATION OF CRITERIA AND PROCEDURE

The Facts

A Home Office Circular, giving guidance to persons in the United Kingdom who wished to adopt a child from abroad, stated that although the Immigration Rules did not allow a foreign child to enter the United Kingdom for the purposes of adoption the Secretary of State would in exceptional circumstances exercise his discretion to allow the child to enter the United Kingdom for adoption if specified criteria were met. The Circular set out the procedure and stated that applicants should enquire of the Department of Health and Social Security as to whether there was any reason for adoption to be refused.

The applicant and his wife were settled in the United Kingdom and wished to adopt a child who lived with its natural mother in Pakistan. The applicant obtained the Home Office Circular and applied for entry clearance. The application, along with the entry clearance officer's report, was referred to the Secretary of State. The Home Secretary did not follow the criteria as set out, but rather those in relation to whether to admit for settlement children already adopted by persons settled in the United Kingdom, he decided that the child should not be given leave to enter.

Judicial review was sought by way of certiorari to quash the decision of the Secretary of State, contending that a legitimate expectation had arisen out of the terms of the Circular. The Home Secretary contended that his discretion remain unfettered regarding the granting of leave to children to enter for the purpose of adoption.

Held

The authority was under a duty to follow certain criteria providing the statement did not conflict with the authority's statutory duty. The Secretary of State could not resile from his undertaking without affording interested persons a hearing and then only if the overriding public interest required it. The applicant would have a reasonable expectation that the criteria and procedure would be followed and in effect they constituted rules for deciding applications for entry. He could only apply different criteria if he first gave the applicant as recipient of the Circular full opportunity to make representations. The Secretary of State had acted unfairly and unreasonably. The appeal would be allowed and refusal of entry clearance quashed.

R. v. SECRETARY OF STATE FOR HOME DEPART-MENT, ex p. LUFF

[1992] 1 F.L.R. 59

CHILD OVERSEAS ... PROSPECTIVE ADOPTIVE FATHER WITH SHORT LIFE EXPECTANCY ... HOME OFFICE REFUSE PERMISSION FOR CHILD TO IMMIGRATE TO UNITED KINGDOM ... PROSPECTIVE ADOPTIVE PARENTS SEEK JUDICIAL REVIEW

The Facts

Two Romanian children lived in an orphanage in Romania. The prospective English adoptive father was aged 53, retired, having had a successful heart operation, with a medically determined future life expectancy of 10 years. The mother was aged 37 and a driving instructress. They inquired of the Home Office who gave them a standard form which stated that on an application for entry clearance, the entry clearance officer would inquire of the child's circumstances abroad and that the Home Secretary would refer the matter to what was then the DHSS for its consideration, if by that stage there was no reason to refuse the application. The applicants inquired at the Romanian embassy and commissioned a private home study report themselves regarding the adoption of the two children as well as advising their local adoption agency, who sought to vet them irrespective of the private home study report they had had commissioned.

Whilst the medical advisers to the adoption panel did not disapprove of the father's health, the Department of Health queried it in terms of suitability because of short life expectancy. That medical adviser changed his opinion even though a cardiologist was not negative. Irrespective, the adoption panel was positive. That, however, would not persuade the Department of Health which confirmed its negative position with the Home Office and immigration clearance was refused. Whilst that decision was subject to a pending appeal, the adoptive parents sought an order of certiorari to quash the advisory recommendation of the Department of Health, believing it to be irrational and misconceived.

Held

The application was dismissed. On one hand it could be argued that the risk should be taken for the adoption to take place as the applicants could be said to be well equipped. On the other hand, the children had already suffered enough trauma by reason of being in their circumstances; they should be adopted by healthy people, being spared the pain of bereavement in adolescence. Both considerations could be said to be humane, with the children's best interests at heart. The advice tendered to the Home Office by the Department of Health was rational and could not be struck down by judicial review.

It was added that the adoption panel was not the *linchpin* of the system laid down by the Department of Health in its Circular to local authorities. It was essentially consultative, its advice being an opinion the Department of Health was entitled to and did take into account, although the Department of Health owed a duty of common humanity to adopters who came forward to help overseas children.

RE VALENTINE'S SETTLEMENT

[1965] Ch. 831; [1965] 2 W.L.R. 1015; [1965] 2 All E.R. 226

ADOPTION ABROAD . . . FOREIGN DOMICILE . . . RECOGNITION OF ADOPTION

The Facts

A British subject domiciled in (what was then) Southern Rhodesia, made an English settlement of a fund on trust on February 7, 1946. The income was to be paid to her son during his lifetime and then, on his death, as to the capital and income, for all or such one or more children or remoter issue as he should by deed appoint. The trust fund was to be held upon trust for all or any of the children of the son in default of and subject to any such appointment, who, being male, should reach the age of 21, or being female, should reach 21 or marry under that age, and if more than one, then in equal shares.

When the settlor died on April 9, 1953, he was domiciled in Southern Rhodesia. The son, also domiciled there, was married with one child. On May 25, 1939 and November 29, 1944, they had adopted two other children in South Africa. According to South African law, an adopted child is the legitimate child of his adoptive parents, entitled to any property devolving on their children. When the son died on July 7, 1962 he had not made any appointments through deed or will. There was no adoption order in Southern Rhodesia because under the law of that country, an adoption order could not be made in respect of any child who was not resident or domiciled there.

Held

An adoption order created the status of parent and child and all matters of statute were governed by the law of the country of domicile, so for the recognition of a foreign adoption order by the English courts it was essential that the adoptive parents be domiciled in the foreign country. According to one view, as the son was domiciled in Southern Rhodesia and the adoption orders were made in South Africa the English court would not recognise the children as adopted; another view stated where that questions arise as to succession under English law, if the English courts recognise a foreign adoption order, the adopted child will be in the same position as if he had been the subject of an English adoption order. In order for an adoption to be recognised, in addition to the adopters being domiciled in the country where the adoption order is made, the child should be ordinarily resident there. The English courts would recognise the two children as the children of the son for the purpose of the settlement.

RE W (A MINOR) (ADOPTION: NON-PATRIAL)

[1985] 3 W.L.R. 945; [1986] 1 F.L.R. 179; [1986] Fam. 54; [1985] 3 All E.R. 449

BRITISH CITIZEN APPLYING TO ADOPT NON-PATRIAL . . . BALANCING EXERCISE BETWEEN WELFARE AND PUBLIC POLICY ON IMMIGRATION CONTROL

The Facts

The appellant aunt was registered as a British citizen in 1975. Her nephew was Chinese by birth and had Chinese parents. His family had moved to Hong Kong in 1974. On October 11, 1981 the nephew was granted leave to enter the United Kingdom as a student for 12 months. From time to time the leave was extended and he had leave to remain to pursue his studies until September 30, 1985. While in this country he had lived with his aunt. In 1984 the nephew's mother had gone to Canada and his eldest sister stayed in Hong Kong but was shortly to be married. His father had died in 1977 and the nephew had no home to go back to. His home for the last four-and-a-half years had been with the aunt. On July 6, 1984 the aunt applied to the county court to adopt her nephew with his and his mother's consent. The Guardian *ad litem's* report supported the application. The aunt's solicitor did not give notice to the Secretary of State of the intended adoption of a foreign national and it is likely that they would have sought to be added to the proceedings under rule 15(3) of the Adoption Rules 1984. The judge would not make the order, believing that the motive was for the aunt to provide herself with a son whose duty it would be to safeguard her in old age; that she was seeking to secure the nephew's immigration beyond the immigration controls, that the nephew was in his eighteenth year and did not need adoption to ensure his welfare from childhood to adulthood; that, finally, the nephew had a perfect natural relationship with his aunt and adoption would not foster love or provide a child with a settled place within a family. The aunt appealed.

Held

Notice had to be given to the Secretary of State where there was to be an adoption of a foreign child or national. If only a short period of the child's childhood remained the consideration of needing to safeguard and promote the welfare of the child carried less weight. The court had

253

also to consider whether another type of order, custodianship for example, might not be preferable. The court had to consider the element of public policy regarding the effect of an adoption order on nationality and right of abode, having to carry out its balancing act between the welfare of the child and public policy considerations. At the date of the judge's decision in 1985 there were only 10 months remaining of the nephew's childhood and for five months his position as a student was secure. The aunt would continue to give him a home if unable to adopt him. The real motives were to safeguard his long-term future as a British citizen with a right of abode in this country and to provide the aunt with a son whose duty it would be to safeguard her in old age and not primarily to promote the nephew's welfare during the remainder of his childhood. The judge's discretion in refusing to make an adoption order was correct.

RE Y (MINORS) (ADOPTION: JURISDICTION)

[1985] 3 W.L.R. 601; [1985] 3 All E.R. 33; [1986] 1 F.L.R. 152; [1985] Fam. 136

ADOPTION ... NON RESIDENT APPLICANTS ... DOMICILED IN UNITED KINGDOM BUT RESIDENT IN HONG KONG ... REQUIRE-MENT THAT APPLICANTS MUST ADVISE LOCAL AUTHORITY

The Facts

A husband and wife both married for a second time. The husband's daughter had two children and the applicants, the husband and wife, sought to adopt them together. The husband was a United Kingdom citizen and domiciled in England. The wife had acquired British citizenship through her marriage to the husband but the children were British Dependent Territory Citizens. The children were at boarding school in England, returning to Hong Kong during vacation, although for shorter exeats and half-terms they stayed with their mother. Whenever the husband and wife visited England they stayed with the husband's daughter. Under what was then section 18 of the Children Act 1975, the applicants had to give notice to the local authority within whose area they had their home. The local authority stated that to fulfil their requirements regarding the preparation of a Schedule 2 report, the wife had to be in England for a minimum of three months and the husband for at least one month, in order to carry out interviews and assessments.

Held

It would be a question of fact in any case whether or not an applicant for an adoption order had a home in England within the meaning of the 1975 Act. There was no obligation that the applicants or child should be living or resident in England at any particular time or for any particular length of time. The obligation was for them to spend sufficient time in a home in England to enable the local authority to see all the parties together in their home environment. The applicants did not have a home in England because when they were with the daughter they were merely guests.

Appendix 6

GLOSSARY OF WORDS AND TERMS

Abandonment

Giving up something voluntarily: a child.

Abode

Right of abode: right to live in a certain country.

Adoption

Act of becoming the legal parents of a child who is not your own. A child adopted by order of a court in the United Kingdom (England, Wales, Scotland, Northern Ireland) becomes a British Citizen from the date of the order if the adoptive parent is a British Citizen at that date. If an adoption order is annulled it will not cancel the child's citizenship. An adoption order made by a court in the Channel Islands or the Isle of Man does not grant automatic citizenship.

Adoption Agency

A body that makes arrangements where one person acts on behalf of another person in contractual terms to arrange for the adoption of a child.

Child

A person under the age of majority and who will not have full legal status until reaching the age of 18: a child is someone under the age of 18 and unmarried for the purposes of the Immigration Rules.

Citizen

A person who has the nationality of a certain country: the British Nationality Act 1981 deals with the notion of citizenship and nationality

in the United Kingdom. There are three distinct aspects of citizenship which can affect the immigration status of a child coming into the United Kingdom:
 i) British Citizenship (British Nationality Act 1981, Pt. I)
 ii) British Territories Citizenship (British Nationality Act 1981, Pt. II)
 iii) British Overseas Citizenship (British Nationality Act 1981, Pt. III)
A foreign adoption order recognised only under common law cannot confer British citizenship unless and until it is recognised by the High Court.

Consent

An agreement that something should happen: natural parents agreeing that their child should be adopted.

Contact

The act of getting in touch with someone: a parent or another getting in touch with a child.

Convention

An International Treaty: Hague Convention on Intercountry Adoption 1993.

Corroborate

Evidence which confirms and supports other evidence: evidence confirming a natural parent's consent to the adoption of a child.

Country

Land which is an entity and governs itself.

Court

The place where a hearing of a legal nature is held: for international adoption purposes, the High Court and the County Court. Where a child has been said to have been adopted prior to coming into the United Kingdom in a country whose legal system is not recognised here, that alleged adoption will be known as a *de facto* adoption.

De facto Adoption

Where a child has been said to have been adopted prior to coming into the United Kingdom in a country whose legal system is not recognised here, that alleged adoption will be known as a *de facto* adoption.

Deportation

Sending of someone away from a country: sending a child from England and Wales who has come into the country without consideration of the Immigration Rules.

Designated Countries

A designated country is a country specified in the Adoption (Designation of Overseas Adoptions) Order 1973 (see Appendix 2G).

Domicile

A country where someone is deemed to live permanently, or has chosen to live permanently.

Family

A group of people who are related.

Foreign

Not belonging to one's own country: a foreign country where a child lives.

Foster

To look after and bring up a child who is not your own.

Guardian

A person appointed by law to act on behalf of someone: a Guardian *ad litem* will be appointed in adoption proceedings to look after a child's interests.

Habitual Residence

The place where someone normally lives.

Immigrate

A move to this country to live permanently: a child subject to an international adoption order will be moving to this country to live permanently.

International

Considerations between countries: treaties are the culmination and the written agreement of considerations between countries.

Intervenor

A person who becomes involved in a case who has not originally been involved: in a sense local authorities could be said to be intervenors in adoption proceedings between applicants and a child.

Judicial Review

Examination of a case a second time by a higher court because a lower court is said to have made a wrong decision, or the examination of the administrative decisions of a lower court: an immigration officer's refusal to allow a child into this country can be subject to judicial review.

Legal Adoption

Where a child has been adopted prior to coming into the United Kingdom in a country whose legal system is recognised here as capable of granting an adoption order, that order will be considered as legal.

Local Authority

Administrators of local areas throughout this country: they are designated agencies for dealing with International Child Adoption matters and must by law be involved in the process of such applications before the court. They can approve or disapprove of any applications as well as make formal assessment reports for the sake of the court.

Parents

The father and mother of a child: where prospective adoptive parents are married they both must seek the adoption order. One of them must be a British citizen. If a prospective adoptive parent is single or cohabiting then only one of the two persons can make the application. That person must also be a British citizen.

Passport

An official document proving you are a citizen of a country: a child adopted abroad or given leave to be removed from the jurisdiction abroad will require a passport to enter this country.

Police Station

The local office of a police force: such a local office must check whether the applicants have any previous criminal convictions and advise the local authority of the position.

Ratify

To officially approve: it is hoped that as many countries as possible will ratify the Hague Convention on Intercountry Adoption 1993.

Registration

The act of having something noted on an official list: when a child is finally adopted such an order must be registered.

Appendix 7

USEFUL ADDRESSES

Adoption Counselling Centre
Family Care
21, Castle St
Edinburgh EH2 3DN   Tel: 0131 225 6441

Adopted Romanian Children's Society
150, Montague Mansions
London W1H 1LA   Tel: 0171 439 4052

After Adoption
2nd Floor
Lloyds House,
22, Lloyd St
Manchester M2 5WA   Tel: 0161 839 4932

After Adoption
The Merseyside Adoption Centre
316-317, Coopers Buildings
Church St
Liverpool, L1 3AA

Barnardo's Scotland
Adoption Advice Service
16, Sandyford Place
Glasgow G3 7NB   Tel: 0141 333 90772

British Association for Adoption and Fostering
40, Shandwick Place,
Edinburgh EH2 4RT   Tel: 0131 225 9285

British Association for Adoption and Fostering
11, Southwark St
London SE1 1RQ   Tel: 0171 407 8800

Catholic Children's Society
49, Russell Hill Road
Purley, Surrey, CR8 2181

Child Care Branch
Department of Health and Social Services
Dundonald House
Upper Newtownards Road
Belfast B24 3SF   Tel: 01232 524769

Child Link Adoption Society
10, Lion Yard,
Tremadoc Road
London, SW4 7NQ   Tel: 0171 498 1933

Community Services Division
Department of Health
Wellington House
133, Waterloo Road,
London SE1 8UG   Tel: 0171 972 4347/4084

Immigration and Nationality Department
Lunar House, 40 Wellesley Road,
Croydon CR9 2BY   Tel: 0181 686 0688

Intercountry Adoption: Social Workers' Group
30, Court Lane, Dulwich
London SE21 7DR

ISS (International Social Services, U.K.)
Cranmer House
39, Brixton Rd
London SW9 6DD   Tel: 0171 735 8941/4

Migrant Trust
8, Musters Rd
West Bridgeford, Nottingham NG2 7AQ

Migration and Visa Department
Foreign and Commonwealth Office
Clive House, Petty France
London SW1H 9HD   Tel: 0181 686 0688

National Association for the Childless
318, Summer Lane
Birmingham B19 3RC   Tel: 0121 359 4887

National Organisation for the Counselling of Adoptees and their Parents
3, New High St
Headington, Oxford, OX3 5SJ   Tel: 01865 7505554

Overseas Adoption Helpline
First Floor
34, Upper St
London N1 0PN   Tel: 0171 226 7666

Parent to Parent Information on Adoption Services
Lower Boddington
Daventry,
Northamptonshire, NN11 6YB   Tel: 01327 60295

Parents for Children
222, Camden High St
London NW1 8QR   Tel: 0181 485 7526

Post Adoption Centre
8, Torriano Mews
Torriano Avenue
London NW5 2RZ   Tel: 0171 284 0555

Public Health and Family Division
Welsh Office
Second Floor, Cathays Park
Cardiff CF1 3NQ   Tel: 01222 823145

Social Services Group
Scottish Office
43, Jeffrey St
Edinburgh, EH1 1DG   Tel: 0131 244 5480

STORK (for ICA adopters)
Dan Y Graig Cottage
Balaclava Road
Glais,
Swansea SA7 9HJ   Tel: 01792 844329

INDEX

Index

CARDIFF
UWCC LIBRARY